HOW TO FORECAST INTEREST RATES

MARTIN J. PRING

HOW TO FORECAST INTEREST RATES

A Guide to Profits
for Consumers, Managers,
and Investors

McGRAW-HILL BOOK COMPANY

New York St. Louis San Francisco Auckland Bogotá
Hamburg Johannesburg London Madrid Mexico
Montreal New Delhi Panama Paris São Paulo Singapore
Sydney Tokyo Toronto

LIBRARY
The University of Texas
At San Antonio

Library of Congress Cataloging in Publication Data

Pring, Martin J
How to forecast interest rates.

Bibliography: p.
Includes index.
1. Interest rate forecasting.   2. Interest and usury
—United States.   I. Title.
HG1622.P74   332.8′2′0973   80-25907
ISBN 0-07-050865-8

1 2 3 4 5 6 7 8 9 0   DODO   8 9 8 7 6 5 4 3 2 1

The editors for this book were Kiril Sokoloff and Christine M. Ulwick, the
designer was Elliot Epstein, and the production supervisor was Paul A.
Malchow. It was set in Compano by ComCom.

Printed and bound by R. R. Donnelley & Sons Company.

Charts 4-1–4-4 from *International Investing Made Easy* by Martin J. Pring.
Copyright © 1981 by McGraw-Hill. Used with permission of McGraw-Hill
Book Company.

Charts 11-1 and 11-2 and Figures 12-1–12-24 from *Technical Analysis Explained* by
Martin J. Pring. Copyright © 1980 by McGraw-Hill. Used with permission of
McGraw-Hill Book Company.

To Danny, Jason, and Laura

Contents

PREFACE

Movements in interest rates and debt markets used to be thought of as a very dull subject in which only specialists dealing in large amounts of money could find any excitement. In recent years the United States bond and money markets have experienced unprecedented volatility; changes in interest-rate levels, which used to develop over a number of years, can now materialize in a few weeks.

It therefore is little wonder that consumers and businesspeople are becoming increasingly conscious of this volatility and are being forced to play a much more active role in the forecasting process. In addition, investors who used to purchase long-term debt instruments in the belief that they were "safe" investments now realize that the risks of purchasing bonds can be almost as great as those associated with equities if the timing of the purchase is inappropriate. By the same token this growing volatility has opened up new profitable opportunities to more aggressive investors and traders.

This introductory book has been written to help such people in their quest for a better understanding of the forces that effect changes in the level of interest rates over the course of a typical business cycle.

The various financial and psychological crosscurrents effecting changes in the level of interest rates are naturally an extremely difficult and complicated subject to analyze over short periods of time, but the basic underlying forces that affect the trend in interest rates over a 2- to 4-year period are relatively simple to understand and can be monitored by almost anyone interested in the subject. It is assumed here that an interest rate is the price of money and that, like any other commodity, the price of money is determined by the interaction of its supply and demand. Although the major portion of the book is therefore devoted to a description of these basic forces of supply and demand as they relate to interest rates over the business cycle, several introductory chapters describe some of the basic concepts, terminology, and the structure of the United States credit markets in the expectation that many readers will be unfamiliar with these matters. The final chapters also show how to put some of the techniques previously described into practice and explain some strategies that can be used profitably by consumers, businesspeople, and investors armed with a rudimentary knowledge of the interest-rate forecasting process.

With this book people with little exposure to business or the investment process should find it easier to identify major interest-rate turning points. While the book will not directly help those trying to time short-term movements, it should nevertheless help them assess whether the overall environment for the credit markets is favorable or unfavorable.

Acknowledgments

I would like to thank Tony Boeckh for permission to reproduce many of the charts from *The Bank Credit Analyst* and *The Interest Rate Forecast,* and Tony Robinson for his helpful suggestions on some of the more technical aspects concerned with Federal Reserve operations. Most of all I would like to thank my wife, Danny, who corrected my grammar, typed and proofread the manuscript, and whose help and encouragement made this book possible.

INTRODUCTION

Perhaps more words have been written and time spent on forecasting stock prices than on any other financial subject, but altogether more people are affected by changes in the level of interest rates than by the movements of stock prices.

This has been especially true in the last few decades, when the amounts of outstanding debt have increased substantially, the level of interest rates has become higher and higher in each postwar business cycle, and the swings in interest-rate levels within each business cycle have become more and more exaggerated.

Although it is often thought that debt markets are a conservative and therefore dull place in which to invest, in recent years the prices of long-term fixed-interest securities have often fluctuated more dramatically than the stock market. For example, in the 12-week period between August and October 1979 a typical U.S. Treasury bond fell by 12 points, for an overall decline of value in excess of 13 percent. In the same period the stock market, as measured by the Dow Jones Industrial Average, lost only 9 percent of its value. Moreover during the longer period between January 1977 and November 1979 the Dow Jones Industrial Average fell only from 983 to 806, for a decline of 18 percent, whereas the U.S. Treasury 8⅜ bond of 2000 fell by 30 points, for a substantially greater decline of 27 percent.

The ability to forecast interest rates correctly has taken on a significance in recent years equal to or greater than stock-market forecasting; swings in interest rates are important not only to the financial well-being of holders of long-term bonds but also to people contemplating taking on the responsibility of a mortgage or installment debt or to a corporation funding a capital project with long-term debt.

This book has been written with the intention of helping individuals, bankers, and other businesspeople appreciate the importance interest rates have for the economy, take advantage of such swings in personal and corporate situations, understand what causes changes in interest rates, and, most important of all, forecast such movements.

INTEREST-RATE MOVEMENTS

Just as the stock markets undergo bull and bear trends, so do interest rates. What is more, in the last few years bull and bear markets for debt securities have become far more pronounced, indicating that private individuals and businesspeople can no longer afford to ignore such movements any more than stock market investors can afford to ignore severe equity bear markets.

The forecasting techniques we will be focusing on are neither highly accurate nor infallible, but studying the forces that propel interest rates will lead to a better understanding of what to look out for at major turning points in the interest-rate cycle. If investors can use this information to improve their personal financial position by selling bonds, deferring mortgage commitments, and the like, or if the corporate treasurer can similarly use it by bringing forward or delaying a corporate-debt underwriting, the book will have served its purpose. The aim is not to pinpoint the exact top and bottom of the interest-rate cycle, a goal that has eluded the best financial brains in the country, but to identify such changes in trend at a relatively early stage, thereby taking advantage of the bulk of a move or avoiding major trouble.

Interest-rate trends can be roughly categorized into four types: secular, cyclical, seasonal, and random. *Secular movements* are very long term ones that occur over a number of business cycles and last anywhere from 10 to 40 years. The postwar period, for example, has experienced an upward secular trend in interest rates as the United States financial system has witnessed higher and higher interest rates in each succeeding business cycle.

The *cyclical trend* is the movement in interest rates that occurs over the course of a business cycle. Such movements typically develop over a 3- to 5-year period. Smaller influences on interest rates are caused by *seasonal* and *random factors.* While it is important to understand the forces acting on the long-term or secular trend of interest rates, our main concern here is with the cyclical or business-cycle-oriented movements, for it is these movements which offer the greatest opportunities for profitable and sound financial planning. They are also the easiest to predict.

The approach to forecasting interest-rate trends will be based on the fundamental observation that an interest rate is the price paid for the use of money and that the price of money, like that of any other commodity, is determined by the interaction between the supply of, and demand for, that commodity. Once this basic principle has been established, the task becomes the relatively simple one of finding indicators that can reflect the supply-and-demand pressures for money fairly accurately. While the task of forecasting interest rates is by no means easy, it is generally simpler than predicting the future course of the stock market, for whereas equity prices are predominantly determined by psychological attitudes to fundamental factors, the level and trend of interest rates are mainly determined by the flow of money in the real (as opposed to the financial) economy. There is never a reason why an investor *has* to buy a stock. Anyone who does not like market conditions can always choose to wait until developments improve or prices come down to an attractive level. On the other hand the federal government does not generally take into consideration the future level of interest rates when borrowing money. This may be a subsidiary consideration, but since the budget deficit, that is, the gap between expenditures and tax revenue, has to be financed, the government really has no choice but to come to the market for funds. When raising a mortgage to buy a house, people do not generally consider the future level of interest rates as the most important factor affecting their decision to buy now or later; they are more likely to be influenced by such things as career developments, family expansion or contraction, or the expectation of the future course of house prices. Consequently expectations can play only a minor and temporary role in the determination of interest-rate levels, the primary trend being influenced by a more predictable and stable interaction of money flows.

We are very fortunate in the United States that the financial and economic statistics which form the basis of our analysis are available not only on a current basis but also have been reported over the course of many business cycles, so that their past interrelationships can be studied and some relatively simple but effective forecasting tools derived. This is not to suggest that all the relationships that have held in the past will continue to hold in the future. Indeed, institutional and other changes mean that they most probably will not. However, if we know what to look for in a conceptual sense and understand that the direction and level of interest rates are determined by the forces of supply and demand, we will be in the position of having a more intelligent understanding of when the cyclical trend in interest rates is likely to be reversed.

While there is no known single technique, and probably never will be, for picking exact turning points, understanding the basic forces that propel the debt markets can help identify a change in trend within 2 or 3 months of major turning points, thereby taking advantage of the bulk of the move, whether it is up or down.

THE SIGNIFICANCE OF INTEREST-RATE MOVEMENTS

Changes in the level of interest rates have a significant effect on the wealth of the economy relative to stocks. The importance of this factor should be considered before looking at some of the benefits which can be gained by taking a more active role in forecasting interest rates.

At the end of 1978 the total value of all the shares on the New York Stock Exchange, American Stock Exchange, and the more important issues traded over the counter was $886 billion. On the other hand the total face amount of United States debt outstanding was averaging $2700 billion, or more than 3 times as much (Chart 1–1).

During the 1973–1974 bear market the value of United States equities as measured by the Dow Jones Industrial Average fell by some 50 percent, or, in terms of capitalization, by about $560 billion. On the other hand if one considers that according to the Bank Credit Analyst (BCA) Composite Long-Term Debt Index, long-term interest rates during this period rose from 6.20 to 8.12 percent based on a 7 percent bond with a 15-year maturity, this would approximate a $220 billion capital loss for all the long-term debt and mortgages outstanding at the beginning of 1973. This of course is well below the net capital loss experienced by stockholders but is still a considerable amount of money. One could also look at the importance of interest-rate changes from the point of view of the changes in carrying costs of short-term debt over the 1973–1974 cycle. For example, 3-month Treasury bills (T-bills), based on a 12-month average, yielded 4.07 percent in 1972. During 1974 the average yield rose to 8.74 percent. Using this debt instrument as a basis for short-term rates in general, we find that a conservative estimate of the total interest-rate cost on United States short-term debt in 1972 was $19.4 billion; in 1974 it had leapt to $62.6 billion. During this period the amount of short-term debt as represented by T-bills due within 1 year, bank loans, and commercial paper outstanding had increased from $478

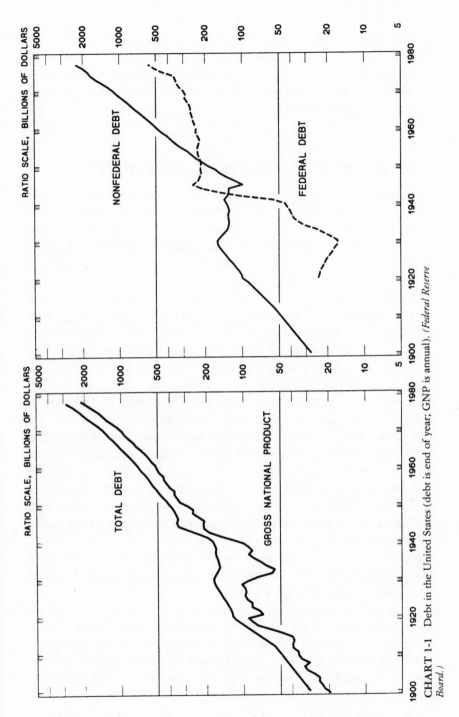

CHART 1-1 Debt in the United States (debt is end of year; GNP is annual). *(Federal Reserve Board.)*

5

billion to $717 billion. In this respect Chart 1-2 on page 7 gives an indi-
cation of the annual increase in money raised by all financial sectors in
the postwar period both in absolute amounts and as a proportion of total
United States GNP. Chart 1-3 on page 8 shows a partial breakdown of
these borrowing requirements.

HOW TO PROFIT FROM INTEREST-RATE MOVEMENTS

Although most people do not like sharp interest-rate fluctuations and the
stratospheric levels we have been experiencing since the mid-1960s and
would much prefer to return to a period of stability, the fact remains that
we are likely to see more rather than less volatility in the future. Interest-
rate fluctuations have to be viewed therefore not as an obstacle to sound
financial planning *but as an opportunity on which to capitalize.*

Because an interest rate is the price of renting money, there are always
two parties to any transaction: borrowers and lenders. Because borrowers
prefer low rates and lenders high rates, naturally there is a conflict. Figure
1-1 shows approximately how each party would ideally like to be able to
play the interest-rate cycle. It also illustrates the point made earlier that
interest rates undergo bull and bear trends like the stock market. To ignore
this fact or fail to obtain a better understanding of interest-rate movements
severely hampers any approach to financial planning.

Let us consider a family intending to build a house or remortgage an
existing home. While generally career developments, change in family size,
and the like make it impossible to defer building, buying, or remortgaging
decisions, it is still possible at times of very high interest rates to save a
considerable amount on interest-rate charges by taking out a short-term
loan and remortgaging the property for a longer period of time later when
interest rates are much lower. For example, on a 12½ percent $50,000
mortgage amortized over 25 years the interest charge over the life of the
mortgage will be $113,000, compared with $86,200, $76,000, and $65,800
at 10, 9, and 8 percent, respectively. Quite clearly there is a considerable
saving to be had by arranging a mortgage at a lower rate of interest. By
understanding the interest-rate cycle it is possible to realize some of these
savings since even though it is unlikely that you would be able to pick the
exact bottom in the level of interest rates, it should be relatively easy to
finance your mortgage at a later date for a saving of 1 to 3 percentage
points.

Understanding and taking advantage of interest-rate swings is also im-

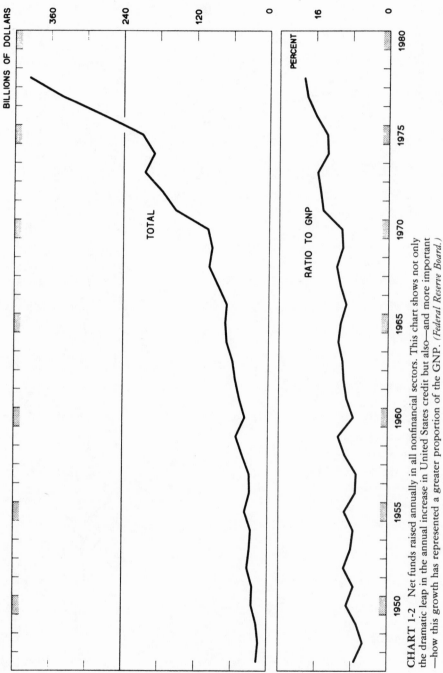

BILLIONS OF DOLLARS

360

240

120

0

TOTAL

PERCENT

16

0

RATIO TO GNP

1950   1955   1960   1965   1970   1975   1980

CHART 1-2 Net funds raised annually in all nonfinancial sectors. This chart shows not only the dramatic leap in the annual increase in United States credit but also—and more important —how this growth has represented a greater proportion of the GNP. *(Federal Reserve Board.)*

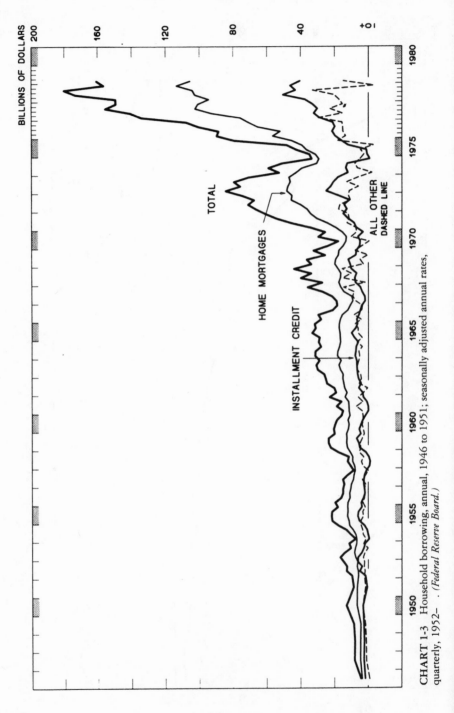

CHART 1-3 Household borrowing, annual, 1946 to 1951; seasonally adjusted annual rates, quarterly, 1952– . *(Federal Reserve Board.)*

8

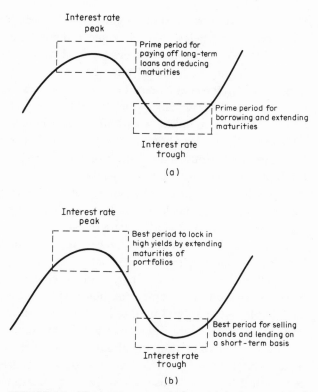

Interest rate
peak

Prime period for
paying off long-term
loans and reducing
maturities

Prime period for
borrowing and extending
maturities

Interest rate
trough

(a)

Interest rate
peak

Best period to lock in
high yields by extending
maturities of
portfolios

Best period for selling
bonds and lending on
a short-term basis

Interest rate
trough

(b)

FIGURE 1-1 The interest-rate cycle from *(a)* the borrower's and *(b)* the lender's point of view.

portant for investors, for when interest rates rise, the value of bond port-folios goes down. If someone holds a bond with an interest rate of 6 percent, for example, and rates in general rise to 8 percent, no one will be willing to pay the investor the full amount for the bond since it is possible to obtain an 8 percent yield elsewhere. Clearly the 6 percent bondholder who wants to sell the bond will have to offer it at a lower price to compensate the purchaser for the loss in interest. It would therefore be a great help to investors if they could forecast the trend of interest rates, for if they knew with some degree of certainty that rates were going to rise, they could sell their entire bond portfolio and put the money into a money market fund, 3-month T-bills, or some other type of short-term-debt instrument and reinvest the money in longer-term bonds when interest rates were on their way down from higher levels. Investors who had adopted this strategy in January 1973, for example, when AAA long-term corporate bonds were yielding 7.11 percent, would have avoided a 16 percent capital loss on their bonds over the following 2 years based on an

8 percent 20-year bond. At the beginning of 1975 the investors would have been able to use their capital not only to repurchase the bonds they had previously sold but because the price had fallen they would also have been able to buy almost 20 percent more bonds.

Moreover in the next 2 years long-term AAA corporate interest rates fell from 8.83 to 7.96 percent, which would have given the investors a 9 percent capital gain on the 8-percent 20-year bonds since falling interest rates add to the value of bonds just as rising rates push them down in price. The dates used to buy and sell in the example were of course chosen with hindsight, but they were purposely selected to occur *around* the time of the cyclical interest-rate peak or trough; while it is a matter of luck to pinpoint the exact month of a peak or trough, it should be a reasonable expectation using the techniques described here to establish such important juncture points several months after they have occurred but on a sufficiently timely basis to take advantage of the major cyclical swings.

Corporations can also profit from major changes in interest rates. For most corporations the volume of business and the level of profits are usually highest at around the peak of the business cycle. When corporations are making a lot of money and are working close to capacity, it is naturally a time to be thinking about increasing plant size. Ironically this tends to be the worst possible time to expand, as it is just before sales and profits start to decline. Also, given the long lead time between the point where a decision is taken and the point where the money is needed, a corporation often comes to the market for funds at a time when credit demand is at its peak, and that of course is the juncture where interest rates are often at or approaching their highs. The corporate treasurer cannot necessarily influence the amount of money to be borrowed but usually has more control over the maturity of newly acquired debt. Naturally it is sensible to finance a plant which may have a life of 10 or 20 years over a 10- or 20-year period, but it is also common sense for this debt to be issued at a time of low rather than high interest rates if at all possible. Consequently a corporate treasurer with a soundly based opinion that interest rates may soon be trending down is far better advised to finance the project on a short-term basis even though the interest cost may initially be higher. When rates are lower, the treasurer can come to the market for longer-term debt using the proceeds to pay off the previously acquired short-term liabilities. To take an actual example, suppose a corporation wished to borrow $50 million to finance a new plant expansion. If short-term interest rates are at 12 percent and long-term corporate rates at 10 percent, the cost of financing the plant at least initially would be cheaper if the corporation issued long-term bonds at the going 10 percent rate. However, the treasurer of the corporation expecting interest rates to fall to lower levels over the next 2 years would be far better off financing the plant with a short-term loan and refinancing at lower long-term rates later on. If we assume that short-term rates average 12 percent over this period and long rates at the end of 2 years fall to 9 percent (a far from unrealistic assumption), the comparison would be as follows:

Finance long term at 10%		*Finance at 12% for 2 yr and 9% for 18 yr*	
$50,000,000 at 10% × 20 yr	$100,000,000	$50,000,000 at 12% × 2 yr	$12,000,000
		50,000,000 at 9% × 18 yr	81,000,000
Total cost	$100,000,000	Total cost	$93,000,000
	$100,000,000 − $93,000,000 = saving of $7,000,000		

Quite clearly the $7 million savings over the plant life using the forecasting approach would be far more beneficial to the company. In terms of an average interest-rate cycle the 10 percent move in rates from 10 to 9 percent is very small. The average between peak and trough in interest-rate cycles during the postwar period has been far greater. Had we used the less conservative assumption of a 20 percent decline in rates from 10 percent to 8 percent in our example for instance, the saving would have been $16 million instead of $7 million.

These are just a few of the examples of how the ability to forecast the trend of interest rates can be used to greater financial effect. While most of this book is concerned with explaining the main forces of supply and demand that interact to influence the price of money, it is nevertheless important to put this knowledge into practice. Consequently some additional examples of a more practical nature have been included in Chapter 15.

Since some readers will be unfamiliar with much of the terminology and technical factors of the operation and workings of interest rates, the opening chapters present some useful background information. Chapter 2 explains some basic interest-rate concepts and relationships, including how yields work, and Chapters 3 and 4 discuss the various debt-market instruments that are available, outline their characteristics, and show how they can be obtained. Chapter 5 covers the historical background of interest rates so that an understanding of the long-term or secular forces that operate on interest-rate trends can be given some perspective.

Although forecasting interest rates can be a complicated process, an attempt has been made to keep the subject as simple and readable as possible so that forecasting can be reduced to a commonsense approach. No resort is made to confusing mathematical formulas or econometric model building since our task is the very elementary one of assessing the demand for, and supply of, money in order to obtain a more soundly based judgment on the future course of its price.

2
INTEREST
AND YIELDS

It is important to understand the basic concepts and terminology (such as yields, discounts, spreads, and so forth) of debt securities if we are to become fully conversant with the technique of forecasting interest rates. These terms will be familiar to some readers, but the fundamentals discussed here will be referred to in later chapters.

INTEREST AND DISCOUNTS

A fixed-income security represents an agreement between a borrower and a lender. The lender agrees to lend the borrower a specific amount of money while the borrower agrees to pay back that loan, usually with interest, on a specified date. In some cases, such as mortgages, the process becomes a little more complicated as the principal is amortized, or paid back, throughout the life of the mortgage so that in the early years the borrower's payments represent more interest than principal, and in the final years the payments represent more principal.

The amount to be repaid is known as the *face value* of the security. Usually the amount paid by the lender (the purchaser of the security) is identical to the face value. In such cases the lender is compensated for the use of the money by interest payments. Occasionally the borrower will receive only a portion of the face value when the loan is granted and be required to pay it off in full on the date the loan is due. In such cases interest is not usually charged by the lender, whose return is the difference between the amount forwarded and the face value. Such securities are said to be sold at a *discount.* For example, if A lends B $90 for 1 year and the agreement calls for B to repay $100, A's return is $10, or approximately 11 percent per annum. The most common form of non-interest-bearing, or discount, securities are United States government securities which have a maturity, or due date, of less than 1 year.

THE EFFECT ON PRICES OF CHANGES IN INTEREST RATES

Because interest rates fluctuate, the prices or value of debt securities also move up and down. For example, if the current coupon rate of interest on a long-term (20-year) government debt is 8 percent, it means that as an investor I would have purchased $5000 of government bonds with an annual (coupon) rate of interest of 8 percent. If for some reason I wish to sell that bond 3 months later, and if interest rates have moved up so that the government could only raise money at 9 percent, it will be very difficult for me to liquidate the bond. After all, why should another investor wish to buy my bond paying 8 percent when one could be bought on the open market paying interest at the rate of 9 percent? In actual fact the only way I could sell my bond would be to accept a price that would be below the face value of the bond and low enough to compensate my purchaser for the loss of interest. In other words, instead of receiving 9 percent in interest, the potential purchaser would receive 8 percent in interest plus a capital gain that would make up the difference.

In bond terminology the face value of the bond is known as *par value* (usually $1000). Prices are quoted as a percentage of par. When my bond was originally issued, it was selling at face value and would have been quoted at 100 (or at par). In this example my purchaser would have bought the bond below the par value, that is, at a *discount.* On the other hand, if interest rates had declined from 8 to 7 percent, my 8-percent bond would have appreciated in price and moved above par to a *premium* in order to compensate me for the fact that I would be giving up a rate of interest well above market levels.

This movement of prices to compensate investors for changes in interest rates, which is a confusing and complicated process to follow, has led to the establishment of a basis for comparing total rates of return over the life of the bond. This total rate of return, which includes both interest and capital appreciation (for discount bonds) or interest and capital depreciation (for bonds selling at a premium), is known as a *yield to maturity.* The immediate rate of return, or the coupon rate divided by the price paid, is known as the *current yield.* If the coupon rate on a bond with 10 years to run to maturity is 10 percent and the price paid is 90, the current yield (10 divided by 90) is 11.1 percent. Since this particular bond is selling at a 10-point discount from par, the yield to maturity would be greater, for it must also take into consideration the 10-point capital appreciation that will take place over the forthcoming 10 years.

Fortunately for investors all these calculations have already been done for bonds of various coupon rates and maturities and are published in *yield tables* (Table 2-1). Bond-yield books are usually arranged according to the coupon rate, the first page listing yields with a low coupon rate and later pages listing yields with higher rates. The example in Table 2-1 shows yields for a coupon rate of 8 percent.

To obtain the yield to maturity for any fixed-income security, it is necessary to know three variables: the coupon rate, the price, and the time remaining to maturity. In our example we have assumed a coupon rate of 8 percent, a price of 90, and a maturity of 20 years. We have already opened the bond-yield book at the page for an 8 percent coupon rate. We look down the column of bond prices on the extreme left of the page and look across horizontally to the 20-year maturity. The circled figure of 9.09 percent is in fact the yield.

Table 2-2 shows another example. Here the 5-percent 10-year bond was selling at a 2-point *premium* so the (circled) yield to maturity was less than the coupon rate.

Electronic calculators capable of computing yields to maturity are now within the means of most investors, and one can do away with yield-book tables, which have become very bulky with the huge rise in interest rates in recent years.

Nevertheless glancing down the yield tables can give the investor a better feel for how price changes affect yields. In Table 2-1, for instance, a price differential between 100 and 95¼ for a 20-year maturity would alter the yield from 8 to 8.50 percent. This difference of ½ percent is known as a 50-basis-point difference, a *basis point* being one-hundredth of a percentage point, or 0.01 percent.

THE SENSITIVITY OF BOND PRICES TO CHANGES IN INTEREST RATES

We are now in a better position to realize that the market value of a debt security is greatly influenced by changes in the general level of interest rates. If interest rates rise, bond prices fall; and if interest rates fall, bond

TABLE 2-1 Bond-Yield Table 8% Coupon 13½ to 30 Years

Price	Maturity, yr															Current yield
	13½	14	14½	15	16	17	18	19	20	21	22	23	24	25	30	
80	10.86	10.80	10.75	10.71	10.63	10.56	10.49	10.44	10.39	10.35	10.32	10.28	10.26	10.23	10.14	10.00
81	10.69	10.64	10.59	10.55	10.47	10.41	10.35	10.30	10.25	10.21	10.18	10.15	10.12	10.10	10.01	9.88
82	10.53	10.48	10.44	10.39	10.32	10.26	10.20	10.16	10.11	10.08	10.04	10.02	9.99	9.97	9.88	9.76
83	10.37	10.32	10.28	10.24	10.17	10.11	10.06	10.02	9.98	9.94	9.91	9.89	9.86	9.84	9.76	9.64
84	10.21	10.17	10.13	10.09	10.03	9.97	9.92	9.88	9.85	9.81	9.78	9.76	9.73	9.71	9.64	9.52
85	10.05	10.02	9.98	9.95	9.89	9.83	9.79	9.75	9.71	9.68	9.66	9.63	9.61	9.59	9.52	9.41
86	9.90	9.87	9.83	9.80	9.75	9.70	9.65	9.62	9.59	9.56	9.53	9.51	9.49	9.47	9.41	9.30
87	9.75	9.72	9.69	9.66	9.61	9.56	9.52	9.49	9.46	9.43	9.41	9.39	9.37	9.35	9.29	9.20
88	9.60	9.57	9.55	9.52	9.47	9.43	9.39	9.36	9.34	9.31	9.29	9.27	9.25	9.24	9.18	9.09
89	9.46	9.43	9.41	9.38	9.34	9.30	9.27	9.24	9.21	9.19	9.17	9.15	9.14	9.12	9.07	8.99
90	9.32	9.29	9.27	9.25	9.21	9.17	9.14	9.12	(9.09)	9.07	9.06	9.04	9.03	9.01	8.97	8.89
90½	9.25	9.22	9.20	9.18	9.14	9.11	9.08	9.06	9.04	9.02	9.00	8.98	8.97	8.96	8.91	8.84
91	9.18	9.15	9.13	9.11	9.08	9.05	9.02	9.00	8.98	8.96	8.94	8.93	8.92	8.90	8.86	8.79
91½	9.11	9.09	9.07	9.05	9.01	8.98	8.96	8.94	8.92	8.90	8.89	8.87	8.86	8.85	8.81	8.74
92	9.04	9.02	9.00	8.98	8.95	8.92	8.90	8.88	8.86	8.84	8.83	8.82	8.81	8.80	8.76	8.70
92½	8.97	8.95	8.93	8.92	8.89	8.86	8.84	8.82	8.80	8.79	8.78	8.76	8.75	8.74	8.71	8.65
93	8.90	8.88	8.87	8.85	8.82	8.80	8.78	8.76	8.75	8.73	8.72	8.71	8.70	8.69	8.66	8.60
93½	8.83	8.82	8.80	8.79	8.76	8.74	8.72	8.71	8.69	8.68	8.67	8.66	8.65	8.64	8.61	8.56
94	8.77	8.75	8.74	8.72	8.70	8.68	8.66	8.65	8.64	8.62	8.61	8.60	8.59	8.59	8.56	8.51
94½	8.70	8.69	8.67	8.66	8.64	8.62	8.61	8.59	8.58	8.57	8.56	8.55	8.54	8.54	8.51	8.47
95	8.63	8.62	8.61	8.60	8.58	8.56	8.55	8.54	8.53	8.52	8.51	8.50	8.49	8.48	8.46	8.42
95¼	8.60	8.59	8.58	8.57	8.55	8.53	8.52	8.51	8.50	8.49	8.48	8.47	8.47	8.46	8.44	8.40
95½	8.57	8.56	8.55	8.54	8.52	8.51	8.49	8.48	8.47	8.46	8.45	8.45	8.44	8.43	8.41	8.38
95¾	8.54	8.53	8.52	8.51	8.49	8.48	8.46	8.45	8.44	8.44	8.43	8.42	8.42	8.41	8.39	8.36
96	8.50	8.49	8.48	8.48	8.46	8.45	8.44	8.43	8.42	8.41	8.40	8.40	8.39	8.38	8.37	8.33

Price																
96¼	8.31	8.34	8.36	8.36	8.37	8.38	8.38	8.39	8.40	8.41	8.42	8.43	8.45	8.45	8.46	8.47
96½	8.29	8.32	8.34	8.34	8.34	8.35	8.36	8.36	8.37	8.38	8.39	8.40	8.42	8.42	8.43	8.44
96¾	8.27	8.30	8.31	8.31	8.32	8.32	8.33	8.34	8.34	8.35	8.36	8.37	8.38	8.39	8.40	8.41
97	8.25	8.27	8.29	8.29	8.29	8.30	8.30	8.31	8.32	8.32	8.33	8.34	8.35	8.36	8.37	8.38
97¼	8.23	8.25	8.26	8.27	8.27	8.27	8.28	8.28	8.29	8.30	8.30	8.31	8.32	8.33	8.34	8.34
97½	8.21	8.23	8.24	8.24	8.24	8.25	8.25	8.26	8.26	8.27	8.28	8.28	8.29	8.30	8.31	8.31
97¾	8.18	8.20	8.21	8.22	8.22	8.22	8.23	8.23	8.24	8.24	8.25	8.26	8.26	8.27	8.27	8.28
98	8.16	8.18	8.19	8.19	8.19	8.20	8.20	8.21	8.21	8.21	8.22	8.23	8.23	8.24	8.24	8.25
98¼	8.14	8.16	8.17	8.17	8.17	8.17	8.18	8.18	8.18	8.19	8.19	8.20	8.20	8.21	8.21	8.22
98½	8.12	8.13	8.14	8.14	8.15	8.15	8.15	8.15	8.16	8.16	8.16	8.17	8.18	8.18	8.18	8.19
98¾	8.10	8.11	8.12	8.12	8.12	8.12	8.13	8.13	8.13	8.13	8.14	8.14	8.15	8.15	8.15	8.15
99	8.08	8.09	8.09	8.10	8.10	8.10	8.10	8.10	8.10	8.11	8.11	8.11	8.12	8.12	8.12	8.12
99¼	8.06	8.07	8.07	8.07	8.07	8.07	8.07	8.08	8.08	8.08	8.08	8.08	8.09	8.09	8.09	8.09
99½	8.04	8.04	8.05	8.05	8.05	8.05	8.05	8.05	8.05	8.05	8.05	8.06	8.06	8.06	8.06	8.06
99¾	8.02	8.02	8.02	8.02	8.02	8.02	8.02	8.03	8.03	8.03	8.03	8.03	8.03	8.03	8.03	8.03
100	8.00	8.00	8.00	8.00	8.00	8.00	8.00	8.00	8.00	8.00	8.00	8.00	8.00	8.00	8.00	8.00
100¼	7.98	7.98	7.98	7.98	7.98	7.98	7.98	7.97	7.97	7.97	7.97	7.97	7.97	7.97	7.97	7.97
100½	7.96	7.96	7.95	7.95	7.95	7.95	7.95	7.95	7.95	7.95	7.95	7.94	7.94	7.94	7.94	7.94
100¾	7.94	7.93	7.93	7.93	7.93	7.93	7.93	7.92	7.92	7.92	7.92	7.92	7.91	7.91	7.91	7.91
101	7.92	7.91	7.91	7.91	7.90	7.90	7.90	7.90	7.90	7.90	7.89	7.89	7.89	7.88	7.88	7.88
101½	7.88	7.87	7.86	7.86	7.86	7.86	7.85	7.85	7.85	7.84	7.84	7.83	7.83	7.83	7.82	7.82
102	7.84	7.83	7.82	7.81	7.81	7.81	7.80	7.80	7.80	7.79	7.79	7.78	7.77	7.77	7.76	7.76
102½	7.80	7.78	7.77	7.77	7.77	7.76	7.76	7.75	7.75	7.74	7.73	7.73	7.72	7.71	7.71	7.70
103	7.77	7.74	7.73	7.72	7.72	7.71	7.71	7.70	7.70	7.69	7.68	7.67	7.66	7.65	7.65	7.64
103½	7.73	7.70	7.68	7.68	7.67	7.67	7.66	7.66	7.65	7.64	7.63	7.62	7.60	7.60	7.59	7.58
104	7.69	7.66	7.64	7.63	7.63	7.62	7.62	7.61	7.60	7.59	7.58	7.56	7.55	7.54	7.53	7.52
105	7.62	7.58	7.55	7.55	7.54	7.53	7.52	7.51	7.50	7.49	7.48	7.46	7.44	7.43	7.42	7.41
106	7.55	7.49	7.47	7.46	7.45	7.44	7.43	7.42	7.41	7.39	7.38	7.36	7.33	7.32	7.31	7.29
107	7.48	7.42	7.38	7.37	7.36	7.35	7.34	7.33	7.31	7.30	7.28	7.25	7.23	7.21	7.20	7.18
108	7.41	7.34	7.30	7.29	7.28	7.27	7.25	7.24	7.22	7.20	7.18	7.15	7.12	7.11	7.09	7.07

TABLE 2-2 Bond-Yield Table 5% Coupon 5½ to 13 Years

Price	Maturity, yr															
	5½	6	6½	7	7½	8	8½	9	9½	10	10½	11	11½	12	12½	13
75	11.21	10.76	10.38	10.06	9.78	9.54	9.32	9.13	8.96	8.81	8.68	8.55	8.44	8.34	8.24	8.15
76	10.92	10.49	10.13	9.82	9.56	9.32	9.12	8.94	8.78	8.63	8.50	8.38	8.27	8.18	8.09	8.00
77	10.63	10.22	9.88	9.59	9.33	9.11	8.92	8.74	8.59	8.45	8.33	8.22	8.11	8.02	7.93	7.86
78	10.35	9.96	9.63	9.35	9.11	8.90	8.72	8.55	8.41	8.28	8.16	8.05	7.96	7.87	7.78	7.71
79	10.06	9.70	9.39	9.13	8.90	8.70	8.52	8.37	8.23	8.10	7.99	7.89	7.80	7.71	7.64	7.57
80	9.79	9.44	9.15	8.90	8.68	8.50	8.33	8.18	8.05	7.93	7.83	7.73	7.65	7.57	7.49	7.42
81	9.52	9.19	8.91	8.68	8.47	8.30	8.14	8.00	7.88	7.77	7.67	7.58	7.49	7.42	7.35	7.29
82	9.25	8.94	8.68	8.46	8.27	8.10	7.95	7.82	7.71	7.60	7.51	7.42	7.35	7.27	7.21	7.15
83	8.98	8.70	8.45	8.24	8.06	7.91	7.77	7.65	7.54	7.44	7.35	7.27	7.20	7.13	7.07	7.01
84	8.72	8.45	8.23	8.03	7.86	7.72	7.59	7.47	7.37	7.28	7.20	7.12	7.05	6.99	6.93	6.88
85	8.47	8.22	8.00	7.82	7.67	7.53	7.41	7.30	7.21	7.12	7.05	6.98	6.91	6.85	6.80	6.75
86	8.21	7.98	7.79	7.62	7.47	7.35	7.23	7.13	7.05	6.97	6.90	6.83	6.77	6.72	6.67	6.62
87	7.97	7.75	7.57	7.41	7.28	7.16	7.06	6.97	6.89	6.81	6.75	6.69	6.63	6.58	6.54	6.50
88	7.72	7.52	7.36	7.21	7.09	6.98	6.89	6.80	6.73	6.66	6.60	6.55	6.50	6.45	6.41	6.37
89	7.48	7.30	7.15	7.02	6.90	6.81	6.72	6.64	6.58	6.51	6.46	6.41	6.36	6.32	6.28	6.25
90	7.24	7.07	6.94	6.82	6.72	6.63	6.55	6.48	6.42	6.37	6.32	6.27	6.23	6.19	6.16	6.13
90½	7.12	6.96	6.83	6.72	6.63	6.54	6.47	6.41	6.35	6.29	6.25	6.20	6.17	6.13	6.10	6.07
91	7.00	6.85	6.73	6.63	6.54	6.46	6.39	6.33	6.27	6.22	6.18	6.14	6.10	6.07	6.04	6.01
91½	6.88	6.75	6.63	6.53	6.45	6.37	6.31	6.25	6.20	6.15	6.11	6.07	6.04	6.00	5.97	5.95
92	6.77	6.64	6.53	6.44	6.36	6.29	6.23	6.17	6.12	6.08	6.04	6.00	5.97	5.94	5.91	5.89
92½	6.65	6.53	6.43	6.34	6.27	6.20	6.15	6.10	6.05	6.01	5.97	5.94	5.91	5.88	5.85	5.83
93	6.54	6.42	6.33	6.25	6.18	6.12	6.07	6.02	5.98	5.94	5.90	5.87	5.84	5.82	5.79	5.77
93½	6.42	6.32	6.23	6.16	6.09	6.04	5.99	5.94	5.90	5.87	5.84	5.81	5.78	5.76	5.74	5.72
94	6.31	6.21	6.13	6.06	6.01	5.95	5.91	5.87	5.83	5.80	5.77	5.74	5.72	5.70	5.68	5.66
94½	6.20	6.11	6.04	5.97	5.92	5.87	5.83	5.79	5.76	5.73	5.70	5.68	5.66	5.64	5.62	5.60

95	6.08	6.00	5.94	5.88	5.83	5.79	5.75	5.72	5.69	5.66	5.64	5.62	5.60	5.58	5.56	5.54
95¼	6.03	5.95	5.89	5.84	5.79	5.75	5.71	5.68	5.65	5.63	5.60	5.58	5.56	5.55	5.53	5.52
95½	5.97	5.90	5.84	5.79	5.75	5.71	5.67	5.64	5.62	5.59	5.57	5.55	5.53	5.52	5.50	5.49
95¾	5.92	5.85	5.79	5.75	5.70	5.67	5.64	5.61	5.58	5.56	5.54	5.52	5.50	5.49	5.47	5.46
96	5.86	5.80	5.75	5.70	5.66	5.63	5.60	5.57	5.55	5.53	5.51	5.49	5.47	5.46	5.45	5.43
96¼	5.81	5.75	5.70	5.66	5.62	5.59	5.56	5.53	5.51	5.49	5.47	5.46	5.44	5.43	5.42	5.41
96½	5.75	5.70	5.65	5.61	5.58	5.55	5.52	5.50	5.48	5.46	5.44	5.43	5.41	5.40	5.39	5.38
96¾	5.70	5.65	5.60	5.57	5.54	5.51	5.48	5.46	5.44	5.43	5.41	5.40	5.38	5.37	5.36	5.35
97	5.64	5.60	5.56	5.52	5.49	5.47	5.45	5.43	5.41	5.39	5.38	5.36	5.35	5.34	5.33	5.32
97¼	5.59	5.55	5.51	5.48	5.45	5.43	5.41	5.39	5.37	5.36	5.35	5.33	5.32	5.31	5.30	5.30
97½	5.53	5.49	5.46	5.43	5.41	5.39	5.37	5.35	5.34	5.33	5.31	5.30	5.29	5.28	5.28	5.27
97¾	5.48	5.44	5.42	5.39	5.37	5.35	5.33	5.32	5.30	5.29	5.28	5.27	5.26	5.26	5.25	5.24
98	5.43	5.39	5.37	5.35	5.33	5.31	5.30	5.28	5.27	5.26	5.25	5.24	5.23	5.23	5.22	5.21
98¼	5.37	5.34	5.32	5.30	5.29	5.27	5.26	5.25	5.24	5.23	5.22	5.21	5.20	5.20	5.19	5.19
98½	5.32	5.30	5.28	5.26	5.24	5.23	5.22	5.21	5.20	5.19	5.19	5.18	5.17	5.17	5.16	5.16
98¾	5.26	5.25	5.23	5.22	5.20	5.19	5.18	5.18	5.17	5.16	5.16	5.15	5.15	5.14	5.14	5.13
99	5.21	5.20	5.18	5.17	5.16	5.15	5.15	5.14	5.13	5.13	5.12	5.12	5.12	5.11	5.11	5.11
99¼	5.16	5.15	5.14	5.13	5.12	5.12	5.11	5.10	5.10	5.10	5.09	5.09	5.09	5.08	5.08	5.08
99½	5.11	5.10	5.09	5.09	5.08	5.08	5.07	5.07	5.07	5.06	5.06	5.06	5.06	5.06	5.05	5.05
99¾	5.05	5.05	5.05	5.04	5.04	5.04	5.04	5.03	5.03	5.03	5.03	5.03	5.03	5.03	5.03	5.03
100	5.00	5.00	5.00	5.00	5.00	5.00	5.00	5.00	5.00	5.00	5.00	5.00	5.00	5.00	5.00	5.00
100¼	4.95	4.95	4.95	4.96	4.96	4.96	4.96	4.97	4.97	4.97	4.97	4.97	4.97	4.97	4.97	4.97
100½	4.90	4.90	4.91	4.91	4.92	4.92	4.93	4.93	4.93	4.94	4.94	4.94	4.94	4.94	4.95	4.95
100¾	4.84	4.85	4.86	4.87	4.88	4.89	4.89	4.90	4.90	4.90	4.91	4.91	4.91	4.92	4.92	4.92
101	4.79	4.81	4.82	4.83	4.84	4.85	4.86	4.86	4.87	4.87	4.88	4.88	4.89	4.89	4.89	4.90
102	4.58	4.61	4.64	4.66	4.68	4.70	4.71	4.72	4.74	4.75	4.76	4.76	4.77	4.78	4.79	4.79
103	4.38	4.43	4.46	4.50	4.52	4.55	4.57	4.59	4.61	4.62	4.64	4.65	4.66	4.67	4.68	4.69
104	4.18	4.24	4.29	4.33	4.37	4.40	4.43	4.46	4.48	4.50	4.52	4.53	4.55	4.56	4.58	4.59
105	3.98	4.05	4.12	4.17	4.22	4.26	4.29	4.32	4.35	4.38	4.40	4.42	4.44	4.46	4.47	4.49
106	3.78	3.87	3.94	4.01	4.06	4.11	4.15	4.19	4.23	4.26	4.28	4.31	4.33	4.35	4.37	4.39

prices rise. The degree to which prices respond to changes in interest rates depends upon both general factors and factors that are peculiar to certain types of debt security.

GENERAL FACTORS

Maturity   The longer the period remaining to maturity the greater the price fluctuation for any given change in interest rates. This is best explained by an example. If I purchase a 1-year bond with a 10 percent coupon rate and interest rates move up by 100 basis points (that is, by 10 percent) to 11 percent, anyone purchasing a new bond will be able to earn $110 of interest. This would compare to the $100 I am receiving. Consequently, if I wish to sell my bond, I must reduce the price so that the potential purchaser is offered a rate of return high enough to correspond to current interest rates of $110. In effect, I have to sell it at a price of $99, which is $10, or 1 percent, below its face value. (In actual fact, the amount will differ slightly from this price because of present-value calculations.)

On the other hand, if it had had a maturity of 10 years, my total return over the life of the bond would have been $1000 or $100 per annum for 10 years. If it is again assumed that rates had risen from 10 to 11 percent, an 11-percent bond with a 10-year maturity would offer a total return of $1100, or $110 per annum for 10 years. In order to compete with that kind of return I would have to lower the price of my bond considerably more than that of the 1-year bond if I wished to sell it in order to make up for the $100 difference above that price level. The yield tables in Tables 2-3 and 2-4 show the actual prices to be about 99 for the 1-year bond and 94 for the 10-year bond.

If the same comparison is made for a bond with a remaining life of 20 to 30 years, the prices would be 92 and about 91, respectively. Quite clearly the longer the maturity the more sensitive bond prices become to any given change in the level of interest rates. Consequently an investor who feels that interest rates are going to rise should shorten the maturities by selling long-term bonds and buying short-term securities, thereby avoiding the risk of a severe price decline. On the other hand, an investor who believes that interest rates are going to fall should take advantage of this situation by extending the average maturity of the bonds in his portfolio in order to take maximum advantage of the anticipated price rise. It should also be remembered that if an investor holds bonds that appreciate in price for a period longer than 12 months, the capital-gain element qualifies for a lower rate of income tax.

The Actual Level of Interest Rates   The higher the actual level of interest rates the greater the effect a given percentage swing in interest rates will have on bond prices. Compare the effect of a 10 percent rise in yields at a 5 and 10 percent level of interest rates, for example. A maturity of 1 year will be assumed for simplicity (we know from the discussion above that the differences in the effect will be even greater for bonds of a longer maturity). Before the rise in interest rates the 5-percent bond will yield $50 to maturity, that is, 5 percent of $1000, while the 10 percent bond will return $100 (10 percent of $1000). If interest rates move up 10 percent, this will mean that the two bonds will have to compete with coupon rates of 5.50 and 11 percent. The actual dollar returns will be $55 and $110, respectively. Thus the 5 percent bond will have to fall sufficiently in price to yield an additional $5 ($55 − $50) while the 10 percent bond will have to fall even farther since it must make up for an even greater difference ($110 − $100). Consequently the higher the general level of interest rates the greater the sensitivity of prices will be for any given percentage rise in interest rates.

The Coupon Rate   The lower the coupon rate the more sensitive bond prices will be to a given change in interest rates. Consider the case of two 30-year bonds both yielding about 10 percent. One has a coupon rate of 8 percent, the other a coupon rate of 10 percent, and it will be assumed that the general level of interest rates declines from 10 percent to about 8.85 percent. Naturally under such conditions both bonds become more attractive to hold in relation to new issues priced to yield 8.85 percent so their prices will appreciate accordingly. The bond with the 10 percent coupon will rise in price sufficiently to bring its own yield down to 8.85 percent, that is, from 100 to 112, while the bond with the 8 percent coupon will appreciate faster from 81 to 91 in order to bring it into line with the lower yield. In terms of absolute points the bond with the 10 percent coupon will rise faster, but in proportionate terms the 8 percent bond appreciates by 12.4 percent compared with 12 percent for the bond with the higher coupon.

Generally speaking, when interest rates are falling, an investor is well advised to buy not only long-term bonds but also (assuming the investor is not dependant on current income) bonds with a low coupon, since they will appreciate much faster for a given change in interest rates. Similarly, when interest rates are expected to rise, an investor would be advised to move into securities with a shorter maturity and a high coupon rate.

TABLE 2-3 Bond-Yield Table for 10% Coupon Rate ¼ to 5 Years

Price	Maturity, yr															
	¼	½	¾	1	1¼	1½	1¾	2	2¼	2½	2¾	3	3½	4	4½	5
90	54.05	33.33	25.35	21.65	19.33	17.89	16.80	16.04	18.41	17.68	17.03	16.54	15.74	15.14	14.67	14.30
90½	51.61	32.04	24.51	21.02	18.83	17.47	16.43	15.72	17.79	17.12	16.52	16.06	15.32	14.76	14.33	13.99
91	49.20	30.77	23.69	20.40	18.33	17.05	16.07	15.40	17.18	16.56	16.01	15.59	14.90	14.39	13.99	13.67
91½	46.81	29.51	22.86	19.78	17.83	16.63	15.71	15.08	16.58	16.01	15.50	15.12	14.49	14.02	13.66	13.37
92	44.44	28.26	22.05	19.17	17.34	16.22	15.35	14.76	15.99	15.47	15.01	14.66	14.09	13.66	13.33	13.06
92½	42.11	27.03	21.24	18.56	16.86	15.81	15.00	14.45	15.40	14.94	14.52	14.21	13.69	13.30	13.01	12.77
93	39.79	25.81	20.44	17.96	16.37	15.40	14.65	14.14	15.11	14.68	14.28	13.99	13.49	13.13	12.85	12.62
93½	37.50	24.60	19.65	17.36	15.89	15.00	14.30	13.83	14.83	14.41	14.04	13.76	13.30	12.95	12.69	12.47
94	35.23	23.40	18.87	16.76	15.42	14.60	13.95	13.52	14.54	14.15	13.80	13.54	13.11	12.78	12.53	12.33
94½	32.99	22.22	18.09	16.18	14.94	14.20	13.61	13.22	14.26	13.90	13.56	13.32	12.91	12.61	12.37	12.18
95	30.77	21.05	17.32	15.59	14.48	13.80	13.27	12.92	13.98	13.64	13.33	13.10	12.72	12.44	12.22	12.04
95¼	29.67	20.47	16.93	15.30	14.24	13.61	13.10	12.77	13.70	13.39	13.10	12.89	12.53	12.27	12.06	11.90
95½	28.57	19.90	16.55	15.01	14.01	13.41	12.93	12.62	13.42	13.13	12.86	12.67	12.34	12.10	11.91	11.76
95¾	27.48	19.32	16.17	14.72	13.78	13.22	12.76	12.47	13.15	12.88	12.63	12.46	12.16	11.93	11.75	11.62
96	26.40	18.75	15.79	14.44	13.55	13.02	12.59	12.32	12.87	12.63	12.40	12.25	11.97	11.76	11.60	11.48
96¼	25.32	18.18	15.42	14.15	13.32	12.83	12.43	12.17	12.60	12.39	12.18	12.03	11.78	11.60	11.45	11.34
96½	24.24	17.62	15.04	13.87	13.09	12.63	12.26	12.02	12.47	12.26	12.06	11.93	11.69	11.52	11.38	11.27
96¾	23.17	17.05	14.67	13.58	12.86	12.44	12.09	11.87	12.33	12.14	11.95	11.83	11.60	11.43	11.30	11.20
97	22.11	16.49	14.30	13.30	12.64	12.25	11.93	11.73	12.20	12.02	11.84	11.72	11.51	11.35	11.23	11.13
97¼	21.05	15.94	13.93	13.02	12.41	12.06	11.76	11.58	12.06	11.90	11.73	11.62	11.42	11.27	11.15	11.06
97½	20.00	15.38	13.56	12.74	12.18	11.87	11.60	11.43	11.93	11.78	11.62	11.51	11.33	11.19	11.08	10.99
97¾	18.95	14.83	13.19	12.46	11.96	11.68	11.43	11.29	11.80	11.65	11.51	11.41	11.24	11.11	11.01	10.93
98	17.91	14.29	12.83	12.18	11.74	11.49	11.27	11.14	11.67	11.53	11.39	11.31	11.15	11.03	10.93	10.86
98¼	16.87	13.74	12.46	11.91	11.51	11.30	11.11	11.00	11.53	11.41	11.28	11.20	11.06	10.95	10.86	10.79
98½	15.84	13.20	12.10	11.63	11.29	11.11	10.94	10.85	11.40	11.29	11.17	11.10	10.97	10.87	10.79	10.72

Price																
98¾	14.81	12.66	11.74	11.36	11.07	10.93	10.78	10.71	11.27	11.17	11.06	11.00	10.88	10.79	10.71	10.66
99	13.79	12.12	11.38	11.08	10.85	10.74	10.62	10.57	11.14	11.05	10.96	10.90	10.79	10.71	10.64	10.59
99¼	12.78	11.59	11.02	10.81	10.63	10.55	10.46	10.43	11.01	10.94	10.85	10.80	10.70	10.63	10.57	10.52
99½	11.76	11.06	10.67	10.54	10.41	10.37	10.30	10.28	10.88	10.82	10.74	10.70	10.61	10.55	10.50	10.46
99¾	10.76	10.53	10.31	10.27	10.19	10.18	10.14	10.14	10.75	10.70	10.63	10.60	10.52	10.47	10.43	10.39
100	9.76	10.00	9.96	10.00	9.97	10.00	9.98	10.00	10.62	10.58	10.52	10.50	10.44	10.39	10.35	10.33
100¼	8.76	9.48	9.61	9.73	9.76	9.82	9.82	9.86	10.49	10.46	10.41	10.40	10.35	10.31	10.28	10.26
100½	7.77	8.96	9.25	9.46	9.54	9.63	9.66	9.72	10.37	10.35	10.31	10.30	10.26	10.23	10.21	10.20
100¾	6.78	8.44	8.91	9.20	9.33	9.45	9.51	9.58	10.24	10.23	10.20	10.20	10.17	10.16	10.14	10.13
101	5.80	7.92	8.56	8.93	9.11	9.27	9.35	9.44	10.11	10.12	10.09	10.10	10.09	10.08	10.07	10.06
101¼	4.82	7.41	8.21	8.67	8.90	9.09	9.19	9.30	9.98	10.00	9.99	10.00	10.00	10.00	10.00	10.00
101½	3.85	6.90	7.87	8.40	8.68	8.91	9.04	9.16	9.86	9.88	9.88	9.90	9.91	9.92	9.93	9.94
101¾	2.88	6.39	7.52	8.14	8.47	8.73	8.88	9.02	9.73	9.77	9.78	9.80	9.83	9.85	9.86	9.87
102	1.91	5.88	7.18	7.88	8.26	8.55	8.73	8.89	9.61	9.66	9.67	9.71	9.74	9.77	9.79	9.81
102¼	0.95	5.38	6.84	7.62	8.05	8.37	8.57	8.75	9.48	9.54	9.57	9.61	9.66	9.69	9.72	9.74
102½		4.88	6.50	7.36	7.84	8.19	8.42	8.61	9.23	9.31	9.36	9.41	9.49	9.54	9.58	9.62
102¾		4.38	6.17	7.10	7.63	8.02	8.26	8.48	8.98	9.09	9.15	9.22	9.32	9.39	9.44	9.49
103		3.88	5.83	6.85	7.42	7.84	8.11	8.34	8.74	8.86	8.94	9.03	9.15	9.24	9.31	9.36
103¼		3.39	5.49	6.59	7.22	7.67	7.96	8.20	8.49	8.64	8.74	8.84	8.98	9.09	9.17	9.24
103½		2.90	5.16	6.33	7.01	7.49	7.81	8.07	8.25	8.42	8.53	8.65	8.82	8.94	9.04	9.11
103¾		2.41	4.83	6.08	6.80	7.31	7.66	7.94	8.01	8.20	8.33	8.46	8.65	8.79	8.90	8.99
104		1.92	4.50	5.82	6.60	7.14	7.50	7.80	7.77	7.98	8.13	8.28	8.49	8.65	8.77	8.87
104¼		1.44	4.17	5.57	6.39	6.97	7.35	7.67	7.53	7.76	7.93	8.09	8.32	8.50	8.64	8.74
104½		.96	3.84	5.32	6.19	6.79	7.20	7.53	7.29	7.54	7.73	7.90	8.16	8.35	8.50	8.62
104¾		0.48	3.51	5.07	5.98	6.62	7.05	7.40	7.06	7.33	7.53	7.72	8.00	8.21	8.37	8.50
105			3.19	4.82	5.78	6.45	6.90	7.27	6.82	7.12	7.34	7.54	7.84	8.07	8.24	8.38
105½			2.54	4.32	5.38	6.11	6.61	7.01	6.59	6.90	7.14	7.36	7.68	7.92	8.11	8.26
106			1.90	3.83	4.98	5.77	6.31	6.74	6.36	6.69	6.95	7.18	7.52	7.78	7.98	8.14
106½			1.26	3.34	4.58	5.43	6.02	6.48	6.13	6.48	6.76	7.00	7.37	7.64	7.86	8.03
107			0.63	2.85	4.18	5.09	5.73	6.22	5.90	6.27	6.56	6.82	7.21	7.50	7.73	7.91

TABLE 2-4 Bond-Yield Table 10% Coupon Rate 5½ to 13 Years

Price	Maturity, yr															
	5½	6	6½	7	7½	8	8½	9	9½	10	10½	11	11½	12	12½	13
85	14.00	13.75	13.54	13.37	13.21	13.08	12.96	12.86	12.77	12.69	12.62	12.55	12.49	12.44	12.39	12.35
86	13.71	13.48	13.28	13.12	12.98	12.85	12.74	12.65	12.57	12.49	12.42	12.36	12.31	12.26	12.21	12.17
87	13.42	13.20	13.03	12.87	12.74	12.63	12.53	12.44	12.36	12.29	12.23	12.18	12.13	12.08	12.04	12.00
88	13.13	12.94	12.77	12.63	12.51	12.41	12.32	12.24	12.16	12.10	12.04	11.99	11.95	11.90	11.87	11.83
89	12.85	12.67	12.52	12.40	12.29	12.19	12.11	12.03	11.97	11.91	11.86	11.81	11.77	11.73	11.70	11.66
90	12.57	12.41	12.28	12.16	12.06	11.98	11.90	11.84	11.78	11.72	11.68	11.63	11.60	11.56	11.53	11.50
90½	12.44	12.28	12.16	12.05	11.95	11.87	11.80	11.74	11.68	11.63	11.59	11.55	11.51	11.48	11.45	11.42
91	12.30	12.16	12.04	11.93	11.84	11.77	11.70	11.64	11.59	11.54	11.50	11.46	11.43	11.39	11.37	11.34
91½	12.16	12.03	11.92	11.82	11.74	11.66	11.60	11.54	11.49	11.45	11.41	11.37	11.34	11.31	11.29	11.26
92	12.03	11.90	11.80	11.71	11.63	11.56	11.50	11.45	11.40	11.36	11.32	11.29	11.26	11.23	11.20	11.18
92½	11.90	11.78	11.68	11.59	11.52	11.46	11.40	11.35	11.31	11.27	11.23	11.20	11.17	11.15	11.13	11.10
93	11.76	11.65	11.56	11.48	11.41	11.35	11.30	11.26	11.22	11.18	11.15	11.12	11.09	11.07	11.05	11.03
93½	11.63	11.53	11.44	11.37	11.31	11.25	11.21	11.16	11.13	11.09	11.06	11.03	11.01	10.99	10.97	10.95
94	11.50	11.41	11.33	11.26	11.20	11.15	11.11	11.07	11.04	11.00	10.98	10.95	10.93	10.91	10.89	10.87
94½	11.37	11.29	11.21	11.15	11.10	11.05	11.01	10.98	10.95	10.92	10.89	10.87	10.85	10.83	10.81	10.80
95	11.24	11.17	11.10	11.04	11.00	10.95	10.92	10.89	10.86	10.83	10.81	10.79	10.77	10.75	10.74	10.72
95¼	11.18	11.11	11.04	10.99	10.94	10.91	10.87	10.84	10.81	10.79	10.77	10.75	10.73	10.71	10.70	10.68
95½	11.12	11.05	10.99	10.94	10.89	10.86	10.82	10.79	10.77	10.75	10.72	10.71	10.69	10.67	10.66	10.65
95¾	11.05	10.99	10.93	10.88	10.84	10.81	10.78	10.75	10.72	10.70	10.68	10.67	10.65	10.64	10.62	10.61
96	10.99	10.93	10.87	10.83	10.79	10.76	10.73	10.70	10.68	10.66	10.64	10.63	10.61	10.60	10.58	10.57
96¼	10.92	10.87	10.82	10.78	10.74	10.71	10.68	10.66	10.64	10.62	10.60	10.59	10.57	10.56	10.55	10.54
96½	10.86	10.81	10.76	10.72	10.69	10.66	10.64	10.61	10.59	10.58	10.56	10.55	10.53	10.52	10.51	10.50
96¾	10.80	10.75	10.71	10.67	10.64	10.61	10.59	10.57	10.55	10.53	10.52	10.51	10.49	10.48	10.47	10.46
97	10.74	10.69	10.65	10.62	10.59	10.56	10.54	10.52	10.51	10.49	10.48	10.47	10.45	10.44	10.44	10.43
97¼	10.67	10.63	10.60	10.57	10.54	10.52	10.50	10.48	10.46	10.45	10.44	10.43	10.42	10.41	10.40	10.39

	10.35	10.36	10.37	10.38	10.39	10.40	10.41	10.42	10.44	10.45	10.47	10.49	10.51	10.54	10.57	10.61
97½	10.35	10.36	10.37	10.38	10.39	10.40	10.41	10.42	10.44	10.45	10.47	10.49	10.51	10.54	10.57	10.61
97¾	10.32	10.32	10.33	10.34	10.35	10.36	10.37	10.38	10.39	10.41	10.42	10.44	10.46	10.49	10.52	10.55
98	10.28	10.29	10.29	10.30	10.31	10.32	10.33	10.34	10.35	10.36	10.37	10.39	10.41	10.43	10.46	10.49
98¼	10.25	10.25	10.26	10.26	10.27	10.28	10.28	10.29	10.30	10.31	10.33	10.34	10.36	10.38	10.40	10.43
98½	10.21	10.22	10.22	10.22	10.23	10.24	10.24	10.25	10.26	10.27	10.28	10.29	10.31	10.32	10.34	10.36
98¾	10.18	10.18	10.18	10.19	10.19	10.20	10.20	10.21	10.22	10.22	10.23	10.24	10.25	10.27	10.28	10.30
99	10.14	10.14	10.15	10.15	10.15	10.16	10.16	10.17	10.17	10.18	10.19	10.19	10.20	10.21	10.23	10.24
99¼	10.10	10.11	10.11	10.11	10.11	10.12	10.12	10.12	10.13	10.13	10.14	10.15	10.15	10.16	10.17	10.18
99½	10.07	10.07	10.07	10.07	10.08	10.08	10.08	10.08	10.09	10.09	10.09	10.10	10.10	10.11	10.11	10.12
99¾	10.03	10.04	10.04	10.04	10.04	10.04	10.04	10.04	10.04	10.04	10.05	10.05	10.05	10.05	10.06	10.06
100	10.00	10.00	10.00	10.00	10.00	10.00	10.00	10.00	10.00	10.00	10.00	10.00	10.00	10.00	10.00	10.00
100¼	9.97	9.96	9.96	9.96	9.96	9.96	9.96	9.96	9.96	9.96	9.95	9.95	9.95	9.95	9.94	9.94
100½	9.93	9.93	9.93	9.93	9.92	9.92	9.92	9.92	9.91	9.91	9.91	9.90	9.90	9.89	9.89	9.88
100¾	9.90	9.89	9.89	9.89	9.89	9.88	9.88	9.88	9.87	9.87	9.86	9.86	9.85	9.84	9.83	9.82
101	9.86	9.86	9.86	9.85	9.85	9.85	9.84	9.84	9.83	9.82	9.82	9.81	9.80	9.79	9.78	9.76
101½	9.79	9.79	9.78	9.78	9.77	9.77	9.76	9.75	9.75	9.74	9.73	9.71	9.70	9.68	9.66	9.64
102	9.73	9.72	9.71	9.71	9.70	9.69	9.68	9.67	9.66	9.65	9.64	9.62	9.60	9.58	9.55	9.52
102½	9.66	9.65	9.64	9.64	9.63	9.62	9.61	9.59	9.58	9.56	9.55	9.53	9.50	9.48	9.44	9.41
103	9.59	9.58	9.57	9.56	9.55	9.54	9.53	9.51	9.50	9.48	9.46	9.43	9.41	9.37	9.34	9.29
103½	9.52	9.52	9.50	9.49	9.48	9.47	9.45	9.43	9.41	9.39	9.37	9.34	9.31	9.27	9.23	9.18
104	9.46	9.45	9.44	9.42	9.41	9.39	9.37	9.36	9.33	9.31	9.28	9.25	9.21	9.17	9.12	9.06
104½	9.39	9.38	9.37	9.35	9.34	9.32	9.30	9.28	9.25	9.22	9.19	9.16	9.12	9.07	9.01	8.95
105	9.33	9.31	9.30	9.28	9.27	9.25	9.22	9.20	9.17	9.14	9.11	9.07	9.02	8.97	8.91	8.83
105½	9.20	9.18	9.17	9.15	9.12	9.10	9.07	9.05	9.09	9.06	9.02	8.98	8.93	8.87	8.80	8.72
106	9.07	9.05	9.03	9.01	8.99	8.96	8.93	8.89	9.01	8.98	8.93	8.89	8.83	8.77	8.70	8.61
106½	8.95	8.93	8.90	8.88	8.85	8.82	8.78	8.74	8.93	8.89	8.85	8.80	8.74	8.67	8.59	8.50
107	8.82	8.80	8.77	8.74	8.71	8.68	8.64	8.59	8.86	8.81	8.76	8.71	8.65	8.57	8.49	8.39
107½	8.70	8.67	8.64	8.61	8.58	8.54	8.50	8.45	8.78	8.73	8.68	8.62	8.55	8.48	8.38	8.28
108	8.58	8.55	8.52	8.48	8.45	8.40	8.36	8.30	8.70	8.65	8.60	8.53	8.46	8.38	8.28	8.17
108½	8.46	8.43	8.39	8.36	8.31	8.27	8.22	8.16	8.62	8.57	8.51	8.45	8.37	8.28	8.18	8.06

FACTORS AFFECTING THE LEVEL OF
YIELDS ON A SPECIFIC SECURITY

Since at any given time specific securities offer a variety of yields, it is important to understand why some issues and issuers are forced to pay higher interest rates than others. This usually relates to the degree of risk associated with an issue.

Credit Rating of the Issuer   The yield differential between securities of identical coupon and maturity but different issuers is known as a *yield spread.* Perhaps the most important factor that influences the yield spread at any given time is the credit rating of the issuer. Quite clearly if there is a choice of making a loan to an institution or individual where there is little or no risk of default compared with one where there is a risk, the loan will be made to the former. The borrower with the greater risk may still be able to obtain financing from another source, but the lender will have to be compensated with a higher yield for taking on the additional risk.

In the United States the safest debt security and therefore the lowest-yielding is that issued by the United States government. Yielding slightly more are securities issued by government agencies which are guaranteed by the federal government.

In order to help investors classify risk, several research institutions have developed bond-rating services, of which Moody's and Standard and Poor's Corporation are the best known. Their ratings, which are discussed in Chapter 3, range from AAA for the highest quality corporate or state and local government debt to CCC for highly speculative debt likely to go into default. The yield spread between the various categories of issuer fluctuates over time depending on temporary short-term supply-demand relationships. Although many bond traders have developed parameters for trading those yield spreads as they narrow and widen, this subject will not be discussed since we are concerned here with general fluctuations in interest rates.

Marketability (Liquidity)   An investor who feels that interest rates are likely to rise may wish to dispose of bonds fairly quickly. If it is not possible to sell them immediately or if too low a price is offered, such a security will be less attractive than one which could be disposed of quickly at a competitive price. A bond that is relatively less marketable is said to be *illiquid* and will generally sell at a much higher yield than an easily marketable one in view of its greater risk.

Obviously an investment dealer wants to avoid holding a large inventory of an illiquid security since in a period of sharply rising interest rates bond prices will be falling. If the security is illiquid, the dealer will have trouble finding a buyer quickly and the value of this unmarketable inventory will continue to fall sharply.

The most important factor affecting marketability is the size of the issue. United States government securities, which are issued in large quantities, are the most marketable, or liquid, debt instruments traded in the United States. Corporate issues with less than $50 million outstanding tend to be relatively illiquid. A second factor affecting liquidity, which to a certain extent is derived from the first, is the number of institutions and individuals holding the bonds. A third is related to the quality of the bond, for clearly in periods of sharp price declines bonds of lower quality offer greater risk and are therefore less desirable even when some compensation is made in the form of higher yields.

Maturity   Normally the shorter the maturity the lower the yield. That is, long-term loans are riskier than short-term loans because the longer the period the loan is made for the greater the chances are that something may go wrong; for example, the borrower may default, or interest rates in general may go higher. Also the longer the maturity the lower the liquidity of any given issue. In other words, longer maturities are riskier than short ones, and therefore the compensation required by lenders is greater.

This concept of rising yields extending out over a period of time is known as a *positive-sloping yield curve* and is shown in Figure 2-1. Yields begin to rise dramatically for the first few years, and then the slope of the yield curve tapers off. This is a normal phenomenon, but at certain points in the business cycle the slope of the yield curve becomes negative (Figure 2-2).

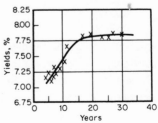

FIGURE 2-1   Positive-sloping yield curve. *(From* The Complete Bond Book *by David Darst. Copyright © 1975 by McGraw-Hill. Used with permission of McGraw-Hill Book Company.)*

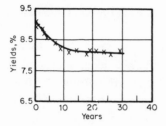

FIGURE 2-2   Negative-sloping yield curve. *(From* The Complete Bond Book *by David Darst. Copyright © 1975 by McGraw-Hill. Used with permission of McGraw-Hill Book Company.)*

The technical reasons for this reversal in the yield curve will be discussed in a later chapter.

Taxation   The taxable status of a security also has an effect on yield spreads. Interest on federal government securities, for example, is exempt from state and local taxes, while interest derived from securities issued by state and local governments is exempt not only from federal government taxes but usually from income taxes levied by the issuing authority on its own residents.

Miscellaneous Factors   There are a number of other factors that can affect yield spreads.

MANNER AND FREQUENCY OF INTEREST PAYMENTS   Most debt securities pay interest twice a year on an accrued basis, but others, for example, Eurobond issues, are paid once a year, making the effective yield slightly less (Table 2-5). Securities sold at a discount with a stated yield have a higher effective yield than those paying interest, since by definition less money is put up at the beginning (the face amount less the discount) although the face value is the same at the end of the maturity. Finally it is important to check the basis of a yield on short-term debt instruments since some are calculated on the basis of a 360-day year and others on a 365-day year.

CALLABILITY   Some long-term securities, mainly United States government and corporates, have a feature which enables the issuer to call or redeem them after a fixed date. Such bonds are usually sold at a lower yield than comparable issues since the issuer will take advantage of this feature whenever rates fall below the coupon rate and use the money to *refund* the issue at the then lower level of prevailing interest rates. The investor also suffers, being forced to reinvest the money at the lower rates as well.

SINKING FUNDS   A feature that is more favorable to the investor occurs as part of the original terms of the offering when an issuer agrees to retire a certain amount of the security. Normally the issuer will pay a specific sum of cash to a trustee who is responsible for looking after the interests of the bondholders. The trustee can either buy bonds in the open market or call in a specific number of bonds by lot, depending upon the terms under which the bonds were originally issued.

The sinking fund therefore has the effect of supporting the price of the bond if it falls below the sinking-fund call price. It also reduces the risk to the investor since the corporation gradually has less debt outstanding.

TABLE 2-5   Table of Annual Yield Equivalents (Yield based on annual compounding equivalent to stated semiannual yield)*

Semi-annual yield	Annual yield	Semi-annual yield	Annual yield	Semi-annual yield	Annual yield
3	3.02	7	7.12	11	11.30
$3\frac{1}{4}$	3.28	$7\frac{1}{4}$	7.38	$11\frac{1}{4}$	11.57
$3\frac{1}{2}$	3.53	$7\frac{1}{2}$	7.64	$11\frac{1}{2}$	11.83
$3\frac{3}{4}$	3.79	$7\frac{3}{4}$	7.90	$11\frac{3}{4}$	12.10
4	4.04	8	8.16	12	12.36
$4\frac{1}{4}$	4.30	$8\frac{1}{4}$	8.42	$12\frac{1}{4}$	12.63
$4\frac{1}{2}$	4.55	$8\frac{1}{2}$	8.68	$12\frac{1}{2}$	12.89
$4\frac{3}{4}$	4.81	$8\frac{3}{4}$	8.94	$12\frac{3}{4}$	13.16
5	5.06	9	9.20	13	13.42
$5\frac{1}{4}$	5.32	$9\frac{1}{4}$	9.46	$13\frac{1}{4}$	13.69
$5\frac{1}{2}$	5.58	$9\frac{1}{2}$	9.73	$13\frac{1}{2}$	13.96
$5\frac{3}{4}$	5.83	$9\frac{3}{4}$	9.99	$13\frac{3}{4}$	14.22
6	6.09	10	10.25	14	14.49
$6\frac{1}{4}$	6.35	$10\frac{1}{4}$	10.51	$14\frac{1}{4}$	14.76
$6\frac{1}{2}$	6.61	$10\frac{1}{2}$	10.78	$14\frac{1}{2}$	15.03
$6\frac{3}{4}$	6.86	$10\frac{3}{4}$	11.04	$14\frac{3}{4}$	15.29
7	7.12	11	11.30	15	15.56

*The nominal annual yield tabulated here assumes semiannual compounding. If interest were compounded only once a year, the nominal rate would be slightly higher. For example, an 8% yield assuming semiannual compounding is equivalent to an 8.16% yield assuming annual compounding.

Furthermore a good-sized sinking fund has the effect of reducing the life of the average bond, which reduces the yield further. The main negative aspect of a sinking fund for the investor arises if the bonds are called by lot when interest rates are at relatively high levels, in which case the investor will suffer the disadvantages of the call feature discussed above.

3

STRUCTURE OF
THE UNITED STATES
DEBT MARKET

The next two chapters discuss the structure of the United States debt market. Understanding the overall structure and makeup of the United States debt system and the interactions between the various components will make forecasting interest rates generally easier to understand. A discussion of the individual debt securities, such as financial futures, will also help to pinpoint some profitable opportunities available to the aggressive investor.

The debt market can essentially be divided into two main areas: the short end and the long end. The former consists of debt with a short-term maturity, from 1 day to 2 years. The long end comprises bonds with a maturity of 10 years or more. Set between these extremes are securities with *issued* maturities ranging from 2 to 10 years, which may be thought of as medium-term. The word "issued" has been emphasized because as time passes and a 20-year bond reaches within 1 year of its maturity, it is still considered a bond rather than a short-term security.

SHORT-TERM INSTRUMENTS

Short-term instruments make up what is commonly known as the *money market,* for since they have maturities of 1 year or less, they are usually purchased with idle cash balances and therefore represent a form of money substitute. Table 3-1 lists the most important of these short-term instruments.

TABLE 3-1   Short-Term Instruments

Instrument	Maturity	Issuer
T-bills	13 wk–1 yr	United States government
Commercial paper	30 days–9 months	Corporations
Repurchase agreements	Usually 1 day, can extend to 30 days	Banks
Money market certificates	6 months	Thrift institutions
Bankers' acceptances	1 day–9 months	Corporations
Certificates of deposit	1–12 months	Banks

T-BILLS

T-bills are short-term debt with a maturity of 1 year or less issued by, and having the full faith and backing of, the United States government. Since the federal government has the ability to support these obligations by raising taxes, they represent the safest form of investment. The sheer size and popularity of government issues also means that there is a ready market for them. It is therefore very easy for investors to buy and sell them in large quantities. A further advantage to holding debt issued by the federal government is that the interest paid is exempt from state and local taxation. Because of these benefits of quality, liquidity, and taxation, government debt sells at higher prices than other instruments, thereby offering a lower yield (rate of return).

T-bills are issued weekly. Most of these obligations are offered with a 91- or 180-day maturity. The former are often referred to as 13-week or 3-month bills, the latter as 26-week or 6-month bills. Newly issued bills can be purchased through a commercial bank or directly through a branch of the local Federal Reserve District Bank. Orders placed through a commercial bank are normally subject to a fee, which lowers the effective yield.

T-bills do not pay interest as such because they are issued at a lower price (discount) than their face value. The yield or return on the investment therefore takes the form of a capital gain, although for income tax purposes this is treated just as interest would be. For example a 3-month bill with a $10,000 face value might be sold for $9760, or a discount of $240. In this case the investor would only be required to put up $9760 and would receive $10,000 at the expiration of the 3-month period. In order to calculate the interest equivalent for comparative purposes, the gain would be divided by the purchase price. In the example cited above, this would be 2.5 percent, that is, 240/9760. Since the 3-month period covered by the bill represents only one quarter of a year, it is necessary to multiply 2.5 percent by 4 in order to obtain the equivalent of an annual rate of interest, which in this case would be 10 percent. Bills are issued in minimum purchase amounts of $10,000 and thereafter in multiples of $5000. They can be purchased either in the weekly (for 3- and 6-month bills) and monthly (for 12-month bills) auctions or in the secondary market through investment dealers and banks. There are essentially two methods of bidding for T-bills in the auction, a competitive bid and a noncompetitive bid. It is possible to obtain a lower price through a competitive bid, but since only a limited amount of bills are offered for tender, the investor runs the risk of putting in a bid which is too low and not receiving any bills at all. On the other hand, a noncompetitive bid ensures the investor of a bill purchase, but the price will be the average of all the accepted bids up to $200,000 under any one name. While bids may be submitted through the local Federal Reserve branch, it is usually easier for an investor to place a noncompetitive bid through an investment dealer, bank, or commodity broker.

Since the bills cannot be cashed before maturity, an investor wishing to raise cash will have to sell them in the secondary market through a securities broker or a bank. Generally speaking, such transactions can be more efficiently executed through an account representative at a securities broker than through a bank.

T-bills are quoted each day in the business section of major newspapers. The following quotation, for example, occurred in the November 20, 1979, edition of the *Wall Street Journal:*

1980		
2-21 ..... 11.92	11.76	12.29

The figure 2-21 refers to the maturity date of the bill, which in this case approximates 3 months. Since T-bills are quoted on a yield rather than a price basis, the 11.92 refers to the yield which dealers will pay or bid for the February 21, 1980, bills, while the 11.76 percent refers to the yield they are willing to offer to you as an investor. One important characteristic of T-bill yields is that they are calculated on a 360-day basis. Since this is confusing for investors who might wish to compare a T-bill yield with that

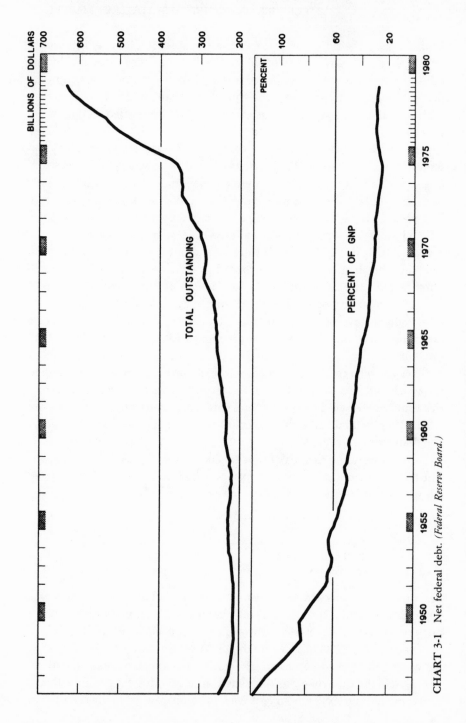

CHART 3-1 Net federal debt. *(Federal Reserve Board.)*

34

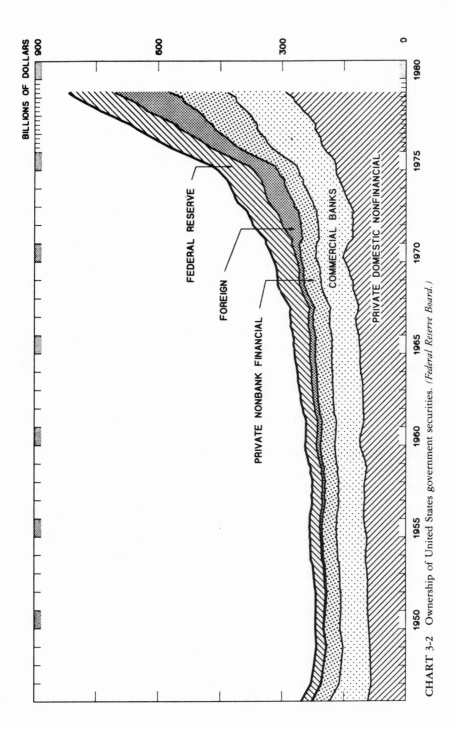

CHART 3-2 Ownership of United States government securities. (*Federal Reserve Board.*)

of other forms of short-term debt instruments, the final figure in the quotation, 12.29, expresses the T-bill yield offered by dealers on a fully annualized basis of 365 days.

COMMERCIAL PAPER

Commercial paper comprises short-term promissory notes issued by large corporations and sold to other corporations, banks, and investors. The commercial paper market developed because certain corporations found themselves with excess cash for short periods of time while others were in need of cash. Normally two such corporations are brought together through the intermediary function of banks, but since the margin or difference between what a bank pays for deposits and charges for loans is quite large, the practice of bypassing the banks grew, so that borrowers could obtain a lower rate and lenders a higher one, in effect splitting the banks' operating margin, or spread, between them.

Although the commercial paper market has been in existence for over 100 years, it is only since the early 1960s that the amount of commercial paper outstanding has expanded at a rapid rate. In 1960, for example, there was $4 billion outstanding, but by 1980 the amount had grown to $110 billion.

Over the years the market has also developed many new participants. Both institutional and individual investors, for example, have begun to purchase and hold commercial paper in their portfolios in view of its higher yield over T-bills.

Since commercial paper is almost always unsecured and represents borrowing done on the basis of a corporation's credit standing, one contributing factor to the growth of confidence, and therefore size, in the market has been the development of credit ratings for the various corporations by credit companies such as Standard and Poor's or Moody's. Standard and Poor's system rates commercial paper as follows:

- A1 Highest investment grade
- A2 High investment grade
- A3 Medium investment grade
- B   Medium grade

- C   Speculative

- D   Expected to default

Commercial paper is usually issued in maturities of between 30 and 120 days, although maturities can be shorter than 30 days and run as long as 270 days. It is normally sold on a discount basis, similar to T-bills, rather than on an interest-rate basis. The normal minimum transaction unit for commercial paper is $250,000. The small investor is excluded from participating in this market directly although, as discussed later in this chapter, it is possible to participate indirectly through the purchase of money market funds.

While the secondary market in commercial paper has improved with the overall expansion of commercial paper outstanding, most paper is usually held to maturity. Consequently investors or corporations who may require to raise cash before the scheduled maturity might consider a more liquid form of money market instrument, such as T-bills, in view of the penalty that would have to be paid on the sale of relatively illiquid commercial paper.

BANKERS' ACCEPTANCES

A bankers' acceptance is a check drawn on a bank usually by an importer or exporter of goods. Unlike a regular check, the payment is not immediate but corresponds to the date on which the goods being financed by the check will be delivered. When a normal check is deposited in a bank, more or less instant credit in the bank account results, but when a check is postdated, the bank in which it is deposited will not receive that money until the day the check falls due and will not credit its customer's account until then. Since it is often inconvenient for check recipients to hold onto a check for the 3 to 6 months in question, banks will accept the check for immediate crediting to the customer's account but not in the full face value of the check. The discount from face value therefore becomes a form of compensation or interest the bank receives for the service of cashing a postdated check.

The bank in question then has the option of either holding the check until "maturity" or guaranteeing payment of the check and selling it to someone else who in turn might hold it to maturity. In guaranteeing the creditworthiness of the check, the bank is in effect putting the whole weight of its own creditworthiness behind it. Bankers' acceptances can also arise where a conventional loan is guaranteed by a bank and then traded in the same way as the accepted check which arose from an international transaction.

Bankers' acceptances are a popular short-term debt instrument with large investors because:

1. They have the full faith and backing not only of the bank concerned but also of the issuer of the check. Moreover many acceptances are stamped or "accepted" by several banks.

2. Yields on acceptances are usually 50 basis points or so higher than T-bills of similar maturity and are exempt from federal income taxes when held by foreign investors.

3. They are available in a broad spectrum of maturities and face amounts ranging from $5000 to $1 million or more.

Bankers' acceptances may be purchased through a bank or securities broker.

CERTIFICATES OF DEPOSIT

Certificates of deposit are essentially short-term loans made by corporations and individuals to banks. They are interest-bearing bank deposits which have a specified maturity. This money market instrument, which is normally issued in amounts in excess of $100,000, has grown significantly in popularity since the early 1960s. Principal and interest on certificates of deposit (CD) are paid back at maturity, which is normally 1 to 12 months. One important advantage of CDs is that they are negotiable and can therefore be traded like T-bills and acceptances. The fact that they are issued by banks themselves also indicates that they are (normally) a safe form of investment. Because of the large amounts outstanding ($95 billion in early 1980) they are actively traded and therefore represent a very liquid investment. The yields offered on CDs are usually similar to those on bankers' acceptances and commercial paper although technical aberrations can push them temporarily higher or lower. Because the CDs issued by smaller banks are usually less creditworthy and marketable, their yields are usually a few basis points higher than those issued by the so-called money banks.

THE LONG END OF THE DEBT MARKET

The long end of the debt market can be divided into three main areas: the federal government, corporate, and tax-exempt sectors. At the close of 1977, outstanding federal government debt (including agencies) with maturities in excess of 5 years was $75 billion, corporate bonds outstanding were $300 billion, and state and local obligations totaled well over $200 billion.

LONG-TERM UNITED STATES GOVERNMENT DEBT

Federal debt obligations trade at lower yields (higher prices) than other bonds because they are backed by the full credit and faith of the United States government and are therefore of the highest quality. The difference in yield between United States government bonds and Moody's Corporate Bond Index has ranged from 20 to 180 basis points between 1960 and 1974 for example. The difference in this spread depends upon changes in the supply relationship between new corporate, government, and government agency issues, investor preferences for quality and safety in any particular period, and so forth.

Longer-term debt obligations issued by the government are *Treasury notes,* which have a maturity of between 1 and 7 years, and *Treasury bonds,* which generally have a maturity in excess of 5 years and often as long as 30 years. Unlike T-bills, which are issued on a discount basis, Treasury bonds and notes are issued on an interest basis in minimum denominations of $1000. Treasury bonds can be purchased like the bills in that prospective investors can make competitive or noncompetitive bids for new issues, or they can be purchased through a securities broker in the secondary market, or aftermarket.

Because of the importance of the government market for other interest rates and the tremendous trading that takes place in these instruments, they are widely quoted on an individual basis in the financial press. Quotations are made on a price basis similar to that described in Chapter 2.

Like income derived from T-bills, interest on Treasury bonds and notes is exempt from state and local taxes. It is important for investors formulating an investment decision in highly taxed states to compare the after-tax yields of a federal government obligation to a fully taxable corporate bond. Once the marginal state and local income tax rate of an individual has been estimated, the calculation is relatively simple, as shown in Table 3-2.

In this example, since the after-tax yield would be the same, the investor would naturally choose the safer and more liquid federal government bond. Investors who wish to make this comparison for yields on bonds with a comparable maturity can use the following formula:

$$\text{Fully taxable yield} = \frac{\text{U.S. government yield}}{1 - (\text{marginal state and local tax rate})}$$

FEDERAL AGENCY OBLIGATIONS

In addition to issuing a variety of notes and bonds in its own name, the United States government also guarantees certain obligations issued by government agencies and other related institutions. The growth of these obligations has been meteoric in recent years. For example, in 1960 there was $8.8 billion of such instruments outstanding while 20 years later this figure had grown to more than $150 billion (Chart 3-3).

Government agencies issue both short-term and long-term securities, and their yields are normally slightly higher than those of United States government securities. For example, from 1964 to 1975 agency securities averaged 15 to 20 basis points higher than T-bills of a comparable maturity, while long-term yields have averaged anywhere from 25 to 100 basis points higher.

Government agency securities basically fall into two categories: those issued by government-sponsored agencies and those issued by federal agencies themselves. The first group consists of agencies originally owned by the U.S. Treasury whose capital stock has been transferred to the general public. These securities are not guaranteed by the government although they do raise money under the Treasury's supervision and are concentrated in the areas of housing and farm credit. In this group are such agencies as Federal Home Loan Banks, the Federal Home Loan Mortgage Corporation, and the Federal National Mortgage Association.

The second category represents agency debt which is guaranteed by the

TABLE 3-2 Calculating Interest on Taxable and Nontaxable Securities

	U.S. government security	Fully taxable security
Interest income	$900	$1000
Assumed marginal rate state tax (10%)	—	100
Interest received after state tax	$900	$900

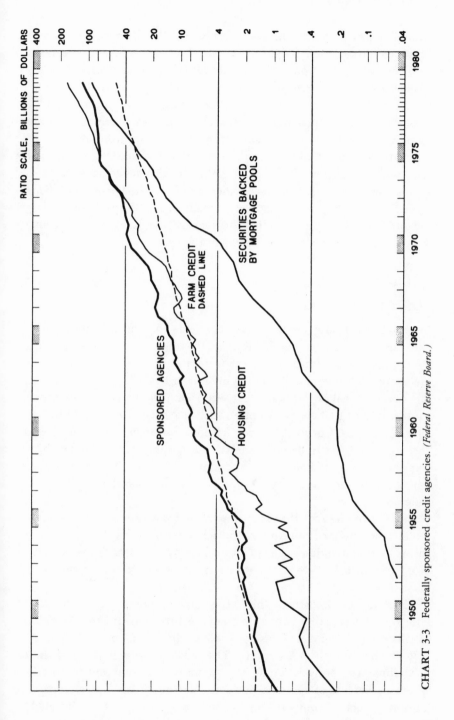

RATIO SCALE, BILLIONS OF DOLLARS

400
200
100
40
20
10
4
2
1
.4
.2
.1
.04

1950   1955   1960   1965   1970   1975   1980

SPONSORED AGENCIES

FARM CREDIT
DASHED LINE

HOUSING CREDIT

SECURITIES BACKED
BY MORTGAGE POOLS

CHART 3-3   Federally sponsored credit agencies. *(Federal Reserve Board.)*

41

United States government. Debt issued by the Government National Mortgage Association (GNMA), Export Import Bank, and the Federal Housing Administration (FHA) would all fall into this category.

New issues are purchased through an agent or underwriting group or by competitive bidding, depending on the agency or the type of debt offered. Details of upcoming issues, such as purchase method, denominations, and so forth, can be obtained from any large securities dealer. These same institutions usually deal in the after market, or secondary market, for agency debt securities. The spread, that is, the difference between the bid and asking price, is usually much wider than for United States government securities since they are less actively traded. Generally speaking, the larger the number of bonds outstanding for any particular issue the more actively it is traded and therefore the narrower the spread.

CORPORATE BONDS

Corporations usually issue long-term bonds to fund a project with an extended life, such as a new plant. Since the interest from these obligations is fully taxable, and since there is a greater risk of default, corporate bonds yield more than comparable government securities (Chart 3-4). This higher rate of return makes corporate debt securities a relatively good investment for institutions that are tax-exempt, such as pension funds and life insurance companies. Corporate bonds fall into two main categories: secured and unsecured. Secured bonds are backed by specific assets owned by the corporation such as land, plant and equipment, and the like. Unsecured bonds are backed merely by the ability of the corporation to continue to generate income.

In view of the fact that it is important for a prospective investor to understand the creditworthiness of a bond before buying, and since a full-scale investigation of its quality is beyond the means or time of most of us, certain firms rate corporate bonds according to their creditworthiness.

The two best known in this respect are Moody's and Standard and Poor's. Highest-quality bonds are rated AAA by Standard and Poor's (Aaa by Moody's). AA and A are also of good quality but not of the unquestionable standard of an AAA rating. The next category is BBB, given for borderline cases between financially sound corporations and corporations where an element of speculation exists. A rating of BB is given when the interest coverage from earnings is very low; a B rating is allocated to

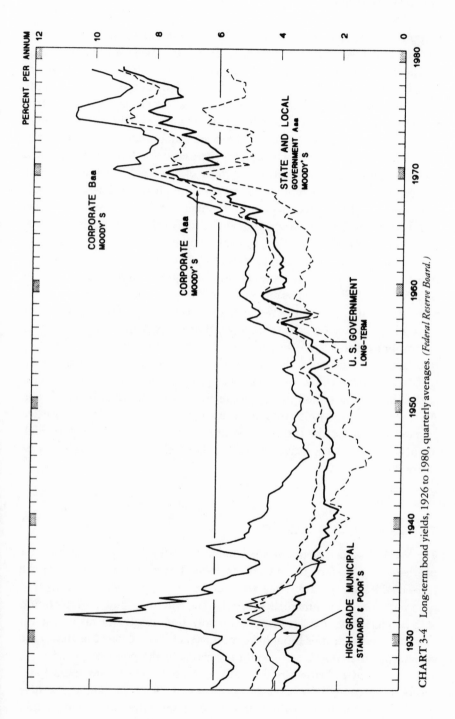

CHART 3-4 Long-term bond yields, 1926 to 1980, quarterly averages. *(Federal Reserve Board.)*

43

corporations where interest payment is questionable during periods of economic softness. Ratings of CCC to D are also given, for bonds ranging from highly speculative to those in the DDD, DD, and D category that are actually in default. The yields on AAA, AA, and A quality issues usually move directly in proportion to other bond-market yields. This is also true for higher-risk, higher-yielding bonds with poorer credit ratings. Movement of their yields is also affected by changing economic conditions. A deteriorating economy, for example, increases the risk of default and therefore forces up yields faster than those of less risky bonds (Chart 3-4).

Corporate bonds are brought to market through an underwriting syndicate which in turn sells them to individuals and institutions. The lead members of the underwriting group will usually call a market, that is, trade these bonds in the aftermarket, but the smaller size of these issues makes their liquidity greatly inferior to that of United States government issues. Indeed very few corporate issues are actually quoted in the financial press, unlike United States government bonds, which are all widely quoted. Some corporate bonds are listed on the exchanges, but most trading takes place on the over-the-counter market, that is, in dealers' offices.

Corporate bonds are often divided into three categories: utility, industrial, and railroad issues. Because of the huge amounts of capital needed to finance such utilities as telephone, gas, and pipelines, utilities have traditionally represented the largest sector of the corporate bond market. As a result average yields on AA utility bonds have come to be regarded as a bellwether for the corporate bond market; not only are they of high quality, but they are usually issued in large sizes and can therefore be easily traded.

THE TAX-EXEMPT MARKET

Tax-exempt securities derive their name from the fact that their interest payments are exempt not only from federal taxes but usually from the taxes of the issuing state. They are issued by city, county, state, and other types of local government institutions such as road and transportation authorities. They represent approximately one-quarter of all long-term fixed-income securities brought to market each year. Chart 3-6 shows the growth of outstanding tax exempt securities in the postwar period.

Tax-exempt securities are naturally of most benefit to individuals and corporations in high tax brackets. As a general rule, tax-exempt securities become attractive to individuals and corporations with a combined federal,

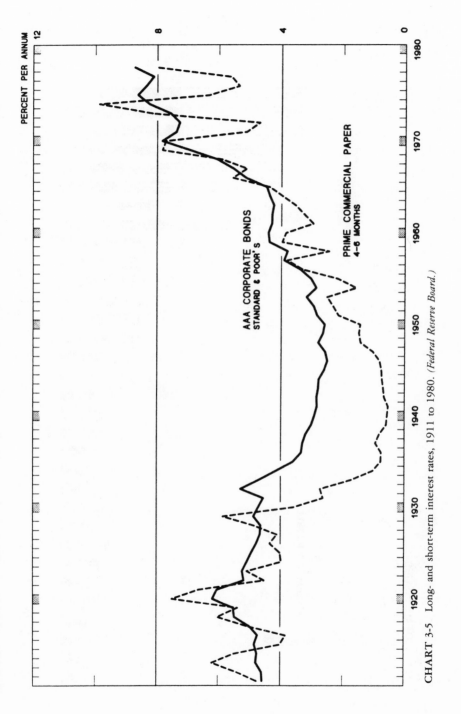

CHART 3-5 Long- and short-term interest rates, 1911 to 1980. *(Federal Reserve Board.)*

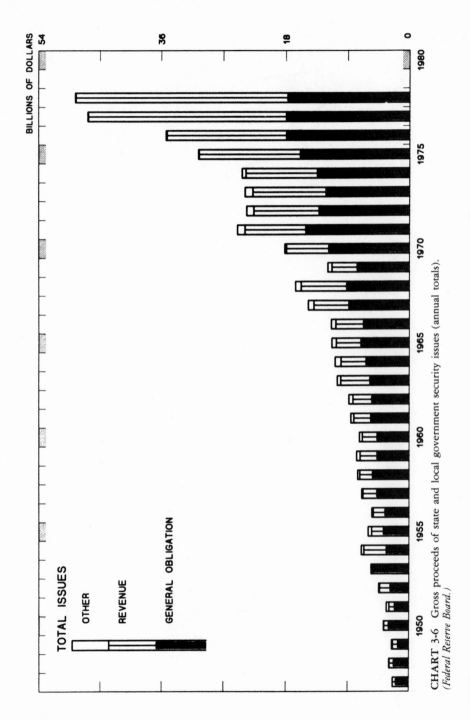

CHART 3-6 Gross proceeds of state and local government security issues (annual totals). (*Federal Reserve Board.*)

46

state, and local tax marginal income of 36 percent or more. The higher the marginal rate of tax the greater the benefit from the tax-exempt securities. For comparison the following formula can be used:

$$\text{Taxable yield} = \frac{\text{tax-exempt yield}}{1 - (\text{investor's marginal tax rate})}$$

Thus a taxable yield of 12 percent for an individual in the 60 percent tax bracket would be the equivalent of 4.8 percent on a tax-exempt bond:

$$\frac{4.8}{1 - 0.60} = \frac{4.8}{0.4}$$

It should be remembered, however, that income tax from exempt securities is not *always* tax-exempt from *every* state and local authority. This point should always be checked before a purchase is made. Second, the tax-exempt status of one city or state is not usually recognized by another city or state. For example, interest on a New York State bond would not be exempt from California state income tax. Finally the formula described above should be used only to compare issues of a similar coupon and maturity since bonds with a higher discount-to-face value will contain a higher capital-gain element in the yield and will be taxed at the same rate for both taxable and tax exempt securities.

While tax-exempt securities possess the obvious advantage of tax preference, they usually suffer the disadvantage of being highly illiquid because of the substantial number of issuers and relatively small issued amounts outstanding. Consequently it is often difficult to obtain a reliable price quotation. Moreover the cost of purchase and sale are much higher because of the resulting larger spread between the bidding and asking price. This factor has grown much more significant in recent years in view of the substantially greater price volatility that has developed.

Tax-exempt securities can be divided into *general obligation* bonds, where the securities are backed by the full faith and credit of the issuer, and *revenue* bonds, where the instrument is secured primarily by income generated by some specific source of income, such as a tax on a specific item or income from a toll bridge.

These securities are brought to market either by an underwriting syndicate or (more commonly) by the tender approach. Because of the variety of credit risks associated with the many different issuers, credit ratings have been derived for them in a manner similar to that for corporate issuers discussed above. Generally under the Standard and Poor's system bonds with an AAA, AA, or A are regarded as safe, whereas the BBB, BB, and

B rating denotes various levels of risk, the highest being accorded to the B rating, where default could be imminent.

Tax-exempt bonds are traded on the over-the-counter market. Interest is usually paid on a semiannual basis, and bonds are sold in denominations of $5000 and up. Usually larger blocks in excess of $25,000 are preferable since the larger size enhances their marketability. Bonds in bearer form, that is bonds which are not registered under a specific name and are therefore fully negotiable, are also easier to dispose of.

FIXED-INCOME MUTUAL FUNDS

In recognition of the fact that many individual investors can afford to buy fixed-income securities only in small amounts and in order to promote diversification, a plethora of fixed-income mutual funds has been offered to the public in recent years. Essentially a mutual fund represents the pooling of the resources of many investors, which are then used to buy a diversified list of securities at competitive prices. In theory the individual investor also has the additional benefit of obtaining access to professional management. The cost of acquiring many of these funds, known as *no-load funds,* has generally been eliminated in recent years so that the only real cost to the investor is the annual management fee, which is usually well under $\frac{1}{2}$ percent of the total net asset value of the fund per annum.

Mutual funds are offered for virtually all types of debt security, ranging from money market funds to federal government tax-exempt and corporate funds.

MONEY MARKET FUNDS

A money market fund is simply a mutual fund that purchases money market instruments. The advantage to the investor of placing funds in these institutions is that a relatively small amount of money (usually $3000 to $5000) can earn the high yield associated with money market instruments such as commercial paper, bankers' acceptances, and certificates of deposit, which are normally sold in denominations well in excess of the means of the average investor.

The money market fund itself earns a return by taking a small management fee usually ranging from 0.03 to 0.05 percent annually. Investors in money market funds find themselves in an unusually liquid position, for not only can they cash their instrument at any time but most funds offer check-writing privileges (usual minimum $500 per check). Moreover, because the funds invest in a variety of instruments, the investor is protected from a total default through diversification.

The risk due to capital depreciation as yields rise is almost negligible since the funds invest only in fixed-income securities with very short-term maturities, the end result to the investor being more or less a very high yielding liquid deposit.

Given the tremendous acceleration in the level of interest rates in the last part of the 1970s, money market funds have grown at a phenomenal rate. In 1974, for example, they were virtually nonexistent but by early 1980 had grown to $26 billion.

LONG-TERM FIXED-INCOME MUTUAL FUNDS

Investors gain three advantages by investing in these funds compared with investment in the individual issues: (1) through diversification the risk in any one security is limited; (2) because the fund deals in large amounts, transaction costs are far less than those involved in purchasing small amounts of individual issues; and (3) mutual funds are relatively easy to buy and sell and are quoted in the financial press.

4
INTEREST-RATE FUTURES

The various debt-market sectors discussed in Chapter 3 were all concerned with cash transactions. This chapter outlines the recently introduced but fast-growing interest-rate futures market.

A futures contract represents an agreement between a buyer and a seller to transfer the ownership of a specified commodity at an agreed price on a specific date. With interest rates the commodity in question is a debt instrument. While there were several types of interest-rate futures contracts trading at the beginning of 1980, there were really only four viable, that is, liquid, contracts, namely, 3-month T-bills, 90-day commercial paper, Government National Mortgages (GNMAs), and 20-year Treasury bonds.

The market for interest-rate futures contracts arose because of the tremendous swings in the levels of interest rates that occurred in the 1970s. Since the economic function of any futures market is to transfer much of the risk of commercial users to individuals willing to undertake that risk, the introduction of interest-rate futures contracts was a natural development. Financial institutions, for example, that wish to lock in high yields on Treasury bonds or government mortgages can buy such contracts for delivery 12 months or more from the date of the transaction. Similarly, investors with a large portfolio of long-term government bonds who expect interest rates to move higher and who do not for some reason wish to sell them can protect the capital value of their portfolio by selling an equivalent amount of United States bond futures. If the bond portfolio falls in price due to higher interest rates, this loss will be largely offset by the profit in the (short) sale of the futures contracts.

THE PROCESS OF BUYING AND
SELLING FUTURES CONTRACTS

Since a futures contract is an agreement to buy or sell a specific amount of a given debt instrument on a specified day, it might be expected that no money would change hands until the contract fell due. In practice the exchanges require a cash deposit to be put up by both the buyer and the seller in case either should default on their obligation. This security deposit, known as *margin,* forms a very small amount of the outstanding value of the futures contract. For example, in early 1980 the margin required on a Treasury bond contract (face value $100,000) was about $2250. While margin requirements can remain in force for several months or even years, they do fluctuate. In the first place the exchange sets a minimum requirement whereas the actual amount charged to a customer will be either the same or higher, depending upon the policy set by the commodity broker concerned. Margin requirements are also changed in response to the volatility of actual market conditions. For example, even though the market value of a Treasury bond contract fell in value from some $90,000 in 1977 to $70,000 in early 1980, the margin requirement was raised from about $1000 to $2250 purely because of the greater volatility of prices during this latter period.

Even with these higher margins the leverage associated with interest-rate futures can be considerable. For example, if long-term Treasury bonds were to rally by 2¼ points above the purchase price and the margin requirement was $2250, the actual gain would be $2250, that is, a doubling of the original investment. On the other hand, a 2¼-point decline would completely wipe out the investor's equity and would either require additional collateral to be put up or would involve liquidation of the contract.

While the potential for gain is considerable, so too is the possibility of a loss. It is therefore important that investors who are considering participating in the futures markets (1) gain experience in the equally volatile but less risky cash markets and (2) ensure that they have sufficient capital to withstand the inevitable buffeting. Margin is usually put up in the form of cash, but most brokers and exchanges also permit the use of T-bills, which are issued in minimum denominations of $10,000. The advantage of using T-bills as part of the margin requirement is that the investor is permitted to earn interest on money which would otherwise remain idle.

The details concerning the four important interest-rate futures contracts are shown in Table 4-1.

Contracts are arranged for delivery in 3-month intervals, usually ex-

TABLE 4-1 Details of Interest-Rate Futures Contracts

Contract	Face basis	Value	Round-trip commis-sion	Minimum price move, basis points	Daily limit move	Value of limit move
T-bills	13 wk	$1,000,000	$75	1	50 basis points	$1250
Commercial paper	90 days	1,000,000	75	1	50 basis points	1250
GNMAs	12 yr at 8%	100,000	75	$\frac{1}{32}$	$\frac{64}{32} = 2$ points	2000
Treasury bonds	20 yr at 8%	100,000	75	$\frac{1}{32}$	$\frac{64}{32} = 2$ points	2000

tending out over a 1½- to 2-year period. If today's date is March 16, 1981, for example, the listing in the financial press for T-bills would reveal contracts for March, June, September, and December 1981, and March, June, September, and December 1982, and so on.

Contracts for short-term interest rates have a substantially greater outstanding value than longer-term maturities. GNMA and Treasury bond contracts are issued in denominations of $100,000, while their T-bill and commercial paper counterparts are for $1 million because of the greater price sensitivity of longer-term than shorter-term maturities for any given interest-rate change (see Chap. 2). In actual practice the changes in the value of these two types of contract are relatively similar, although it should be noted that short- and long-term interest rates do not necessarily move either to the same degree or even in the same direction for any given economic or financial development.

The futures contract for 90-day T-bills and commercial paper calls for par (100) delivery of the face value of $1 million at maturity. The actual price of these contracts is quoted in terms of an index devised by the exchange. This index represents the annualized interest yield subtracted from 100. Thus an index number of 95 indicates an annual yield of 5 percent, 85 a yield of 15 percent, etc. The contract appreciates in value as the prices go up, that is, interest rates fall. A price change of 1 basis point alters the value of the contract by $25 and 100 basis points (one full percentage point) by $2500.

GNMA and Treasury bonds, on the other hand, are priced in the same way as long-term bonds. Fractions of a point are expressed as thirty-seconds. Each one-thirty-second point move alters the value of the contract by $31.25. A movement of 1 full percentage point, on the other hand, has the effect of raising or lowering the value of the contract by $1000.

When trading in a new delivery month begins, there are no contracts in existence. Contracts can be created only when a buyer and seller complete a transaction. The number of contracts outstanding at any particular time is known as the *open interest.*

FUTURES VERSUS THE CASH MARKET

The possibilities of the greater available leverage of the futures markets vis à vis the cash market have already been discussed, but there are other important differences as well. In the cash market some form of delivery of the debt instrument in question always results from a transaction. Futures contracts, on the other hand, are often created where the buyer, the seller, or both have no intention of giving or taking delivery of the actual certificate. Such transactions are speculative in nature and greatly influence the open-interest figure. Generally speaking, a rising market should be accompanied by an expanding open interest and a falling one by a declining open interest. Sometimes the open interest rises dramatically with the price over the relatively short period of a few days or a week. Such moves generally indicate an emotional buying reaction and should be treated with the utmost caution. On the other hand, a protracted decline in prices accompanied by a significant falloff in the open interest is often a sign of genuine discouragement and pessimism. When this happens and the economic, financial, and technical factors discussed in later chapters are in place, it is normally safe to assume that a major buying opportunity is at hand.

From a capital-gains point of view, an investment in interest-rate futures contracts has two distinct advantages over a similar investment in the cash market: (1) as discussed above, it is possible to obtain far greater leverage and therefore potential gain (if you are right) because of the smaller margin requirement, and (2) it is easier to capitalize on periods in which interest rates are rising, that is, the prices of debt instruments are falling. This is because the procedure for selling an interest-rate futures contract is just as easy as for buying. The seller simply puts up the margin and sells the contract. If the seller is correct and prices fall, the seller then buys back the contract at an appropriate time and pockets the difference between the higher selling price and the lower purchase price. All that has happened is that the procedure of buying and selling has been reversed. This process of selling a contract, the instrument for which one does not own or intend to own, is called *short selling.*

Normally the major movement of the cash and futures prices will be relatively close, but since expectations play a more significant part in the pricing of futures contracts, from time to time there are diverging trends between the far-out (deferred) contracts and the nearby ones. If, for example, during a cyclical rise in interest rates participants in the futures markets were anticipating a peak in yields 12 months hence but new evidence caused a change by bringing forward those expectations by 6 months, there would be a change in the price of the far-out contracts even though the spot rate remained basically the same. Differences between the nearby and deferred options can also develop as a result of alterations in the yield curve of the cash market, which opens up arbitrage possibilities in the futures market. (*Arbitrage* is the process of taking advantage of price discrepancies of an identical asset in two markets by buying in one market and selling in the other.)

An example of changing expectations and their influence on the future markets occurred in mid-1979. Charts 4-1 to 4-4 reflect the price changes of four T-bill futures contracts between late 1978 and early 1979. Reference to these charts shows that in February 1979 each of the contracts was around the 90.5 level. Although there was a slight discrepancy between their movements over the following months, it was not until May that a

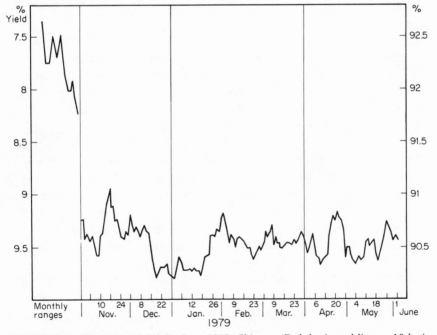

CHART 4-1   Thirteen-week T-bills, June 1979, Chicago. (Each horizontal line = 10 basis points.)

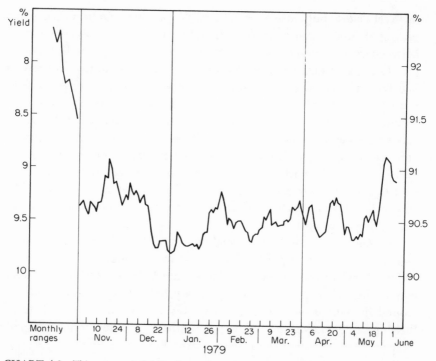

CHART 4-2 Thirteen-week T-bills, September 1979, Chicago. (Each horizontal line = 10 basis points.)

significant alteration in expectations developed as the prices of the deferred contracts moved up substantially more than in the nearby months. It is also worth noting that throughout this period the cash market for 90-day T-bills remained relatively unchanged although some of the far-out contracts moved up by as much as 100 points.

This type of dramatic swing is unusual, but it points out the fact that the relationship between the cash and the futures market is not always identical and that positions in far-out contracts should be based on an analysis of both the price action and fundamental background affecting these contracts and those of the cash market. It is also worth noting that market expectations can often be wrong. The example cited above, for instance, suggested that market participants were looking for a relatively early peak in interest rates. As it turned out, the eventual cyclical peak occurred far later and at significantly higher yields than those anticipated by the markets.

Investors in interest-rate futures who wish to follow the primary or cyclical trend in interest rates can minimize these problems of second guessing the expectations of futures markets participants by investing in the nearby contracts (3- to 6-month futures), which will be considerably less subject to such distortions. Positions can be maintained by rolling the contract over into the new nearby position just before the expiration of the old one. One disadvantage to this procedure arises from the tax treatment of capital gains achieved in the futures markets: Capital gains in the commodity markets which are realized within a 6-month holding period are classified as ordinary income for tax purposes, whereas gains realized over a longer period are treated as capital gains for tax purposes and therefore qualify for the reduced rate. This problem does not arise from short positions since profits derived from such transactions are all treated as ordinary income for tax purposes regardless of the length of time over which they were made.

A further difference between interest-rate futures contracts and the cash market is that on rare occasions an unexpected economic, financial, or political development may have a very significant effect on the price level. Whereas the cash price adjusts almost simultaneously, the futures market often cannot because the various exchanges post a limit on how much the price of each contract may move in a particular day. Limit moves for the specific contracts are listed in Table 4-1. This problem of being

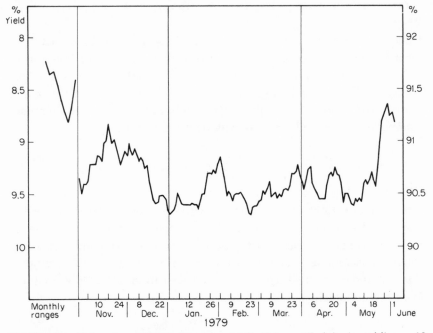

CHART 4-3   Thirteen-week T-bills, December 1979, Chicago. (Each horizontal line = 10 basis points.)

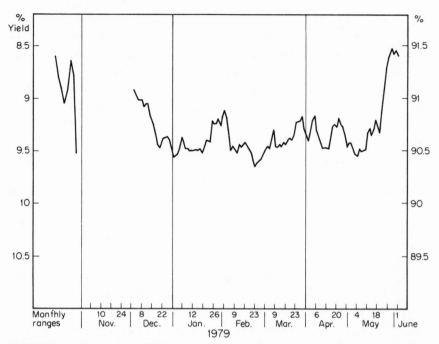

CHART 4-4 Thirteen-week T-bills, March 1980, Chicago. (Each horizontal line = 10 basis points.)

locked in does not occur very often, but it is an additional risk factor that must be taken into consideration when dealing with these investments. Like margin requirements and other details presented in Table 4-1, limit moves are subject to change depending on the volatility of the specific markets concerned. Current particulars can be obtained from any reputable commodity dealer selling these new debt instruments.

SUMMARY

Interest-rate futures contracts are a relatively new and leveraged way to play the bond and money markets. Since leverage works both ways, investors are strongly advised not to approach these markets until they have gained considerable experience from the cash markets. All futures positions should be backed up with capital well in excess of the minimum margin requirements.

5
INTEREST RATES
IN PERSPECTIVE

Most of us judge the level of interest rates by the experience of our own lifetime. For instance, in the 1950s rates were generally below 4 percent, which was considered to be normal at the time. On the other hand, by the late 1970s interest rates had reached the kind of double-digit numbers which would have been unthinkable to investors in the early postwar period. These examples are used to suggest that one should not come away with preconceived views of what is and what is not a high or low level of interest. It is a fact that almost every generation is at some point greatly surprised by the course of interest rates, for in recorded history interest-rate trends have rarely been stable for long periods of time.

Sidney Homer* points out that the highest and lowest rates in recorded history occurred in this century. The high occurred in Berlin in the 1920s at 10,000 percent and the lowest in New York at 0.1 percent. Both were standard money market quotations, but each was made under special circumstances, one during a hyperinflation and the other during a period of deflation. While they are unlikely to be repeated, the fact that they happened at all shows that it is not inconceivable for rates to rise and fall significantly above or below the accepted standards of the day.

Chart 5-1 shows the level of interest rates for Babylonia, Greece, and Rome. It should be pointed out that the data from which this chart was compiled are very shaky since they have been taken from sporadic references. Even though many of the data have been corroborated from other sources, they should still be treated with caution. What does appear to be verifiable, however, is the overall trend during these periods. For example,

*The History of Interest Rates, Rutgers University Press, New Brunswick, N.J., 1963.

the trend of both Greek and Roman interest rates was a declining one before the Christian era. In the first century BC Roman rates had fallen as low as 4 percent, almost the lowest in recorded ancient history. From about AD 100 rates began to rise as inflation accelerated as a result of the debasement of the currency.

What is apparent from the trend of interest rates in each of these series is that rates appear to have traced out a saucerlike formation as they initially fall, then move sideways, and eventually rise. The final rise probably characterizes the terminal phase of each state, which is typically associated with currency debasement and substantial price inflation as the weakened political structure causes the authorities to take the easy way out of solving their problems by coining more money.

While the data on ancient interest rates are very sporadic, it can still be seen that their levels fluctuated greatly throughout this period, as they have over long periods ever since.

THE FOUR FORCES OPERATING ON INTEREST-RATE TRENDS

There are essentially four forces acting on interest rates during any one period: the very long run (or secular), the cyclical, the seasonal, and the random.

In reverse order, the random force occurs as the result of some dramatic event such as the outbreak of war, a major change in government policy, an unexpected crisis, and so on.

Seasonal factors affect interest rates over a much shorter period than cyclical or secular factors. For example, the demand for money is greater during October and November as retailers build up inventories for the peak Christmas period. As Christmas sales develop, inventories are run down and interest rates decline. Thus there is a tendency for rates to fall during October to January. In recent years governments have attempted to cushion these and other seasonal tendencies by putting money in or taking it out of the system, whichever is appropriate.

Cyclical forces operate over the typical business cycle, which can extend for 2 to 5 years.

Essentially the cyclical movement of interest rates develops as follows. Interest rates reach their peak as the economy enters or has just entered a recession, since this is normally the point at which economic and financial capacity are at their tightest. As the recession unfolds, business weakens and the supply-demand relationship of credit moves in favor of the

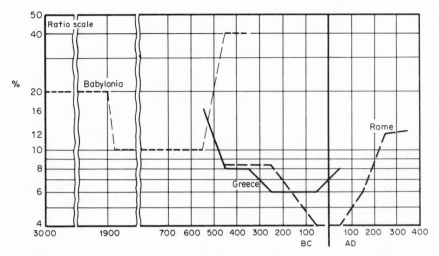

CHART 5-1   Ancient interest rates. Long-term trends of minimum interest rates in Babylonia, Greece, and Rome. The lowest rate reported for each area in each period; all presumably related to short-term loans. Minimum Greek rates were substantially all Athenian rates. Babylonian and Roman rates at their higher levels were usually legal maxima, but at their lowest levels were far below legal maxima. *(From Sidney Homer,* The History of Interest Rates, *Rutgers University Press, Rutgers, N.J., 1963.)*

supply side, so that rates decline. Only when the economy is well into the recovery stage does the demand for money overtake its supply, causing rates to rise. The cyclical movement of interest from an investment point of view is the most important and is covered in greater detail in several subsequent chapters. The secular forces are those which operate over a number of business cycles and can last from 10 to 50 years, and is the area on which the remainder of this chapter concentrates. Most people over the age of thirty are aware that the trend of interest rates in the postwar period has been a rising one. Each cyclical peak has been higher than its predecessor, as has each trough. Chart 3-5 shows this quite clearly. It also shows that during the 1930s and 1940s the long-term secular trend was quite different since rates were declining during this period.

From the point of view of forecasting interest rates over the course of a business cycle it is very important to understand the direction of the secular trend, which will have a significant influence not only on the level of the interest-rate peaks and troughs but also on the duration of the various cyclical bull and bear markets. For example, during the postwar period interest rates have been in an essentially rising phase interrupted by generally small bull markets as rates have declined. On the other hand, it was the bear markets in the 1930s and 1940s that were relatively short-lived. An appreciation of the secular trend can therefore give the investor a far better perspective on the kind of cyclical movement to be expected.

This long-term or secular cycle has been called the 50- to 54-year cycle or the *Kondratieff wave* (after the Russian economist Nicolai Kondratieff). Two other important long-term cycles that have an effect on the cyclical movement of interest rates are the 9.2-year *(Juglar)* and 18⅓-year cycles. Their influence is also important to the duration and timing of the 3- to 4-year business cycle, also known as the *Kitchin cycle.*

The interaction of three of these cycles is shown in Chart 5-2. The large dashed-dotted curve shows the summation of each of these cycles (Kondratieff, Juglar, and Kitchin) as calculated by Schumpeter. A comparison of this chart with Chart 3-5 shows how the upward phase of his long-term cycle has been associated with rising interest rates throughout the postwar period.

THE KONDRATIEFF LONG WAVE

Nicolai Kondratieff observed that the United States economy had undergone three complete waves since its inception, each wave lasting approximately 50 to 54 years (Kondratieff was not the only economist to note the cycle; Jevons also referred to it in the latter part of the nineteenth century). E. H. Phelps Brown and Sheila Hopkins, of the London School of Economics, have noticed the recurrence of a regular 50- to 52-year cycle of prices in the United Kingdom between 1271 and 1954. Chart 5-3 represents the interaction between wholesale prices and an idealized Kondratieff wave. (Chart 5-4 shows actual interest-rate movements during the same Kondratieff cycle.)

Kondratieff used wholesale prices, not interest rates, as the central point

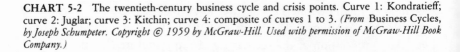

CHART 5-2   The twentieth-century business cycle and crisis points. Curve 1: Kondratieff; curve 2: Juglar; curve 3: Kitchin; curve 4: composite of curves 1 to 3. *(From* Business Cycles, *by Joseph Schumpeter. Copyright © 1959 by McGraw-Hill. Used with permission of McGraw-Hill Book Company.)*

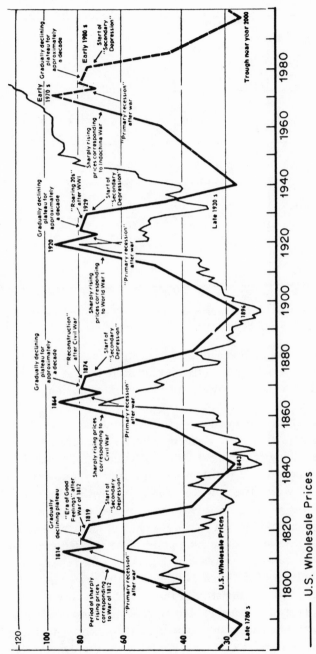

— U.S. Wholesale Prices

— Idealized Kondratieff Wave

CHART 5-3   The Kondratieff wave.

Yield (%)

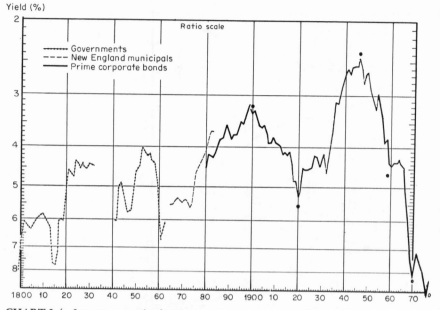

CHART 5-4   Long-term trends of interest rates. Annual averages. Dots indicate monthly high or low yields at cyclical turning points for this century. *(Salomon Brothers.)*

for his theory. As we shall discover in later chapters, however, there is a strong relationship between interest rates and inflation, so that the long-term trend of interest rates falls quite conveniently into this long-wave theory.

Kondratieff's basic theory is shown in graphic form in Chart 5-3. Reference to the chart shows that each wave in wholesale prices has three phases. An upwave lasting for approximately 20 years is followed by a transition or plateau period of 7 to 10 years and finally by a downwave lasting again about 20 years. The upwave is associated with rising prices (and interest rates), the plateau period with stable prices, and the downwave with falling prices (and interest rates). Kondratieff also noted that a war was associated with the major turning points. The war at the top of the cycle, when interest rates and prices were highest, is called the *peak war* and the one at the bottom of the cycle is known as the *trough war*.

Kondratieff observed that at the start of the cycle business conditions are very depressed. There is a considerable amount of spare capacity in both the economic and financial systems. In effect plants and equipment are operating at very low rates of capacity, and since the demand for money is very low, there is plenty avaliable for loans. Fear and poor investment conditions encourage people to save rather than invest. At such periods of surplus liquidity, interest rates are close to their extreme secular lows, as the conditions of the 1930s and 1940s testify. Gradually interest rates fall so much that corporations are encouraged to borrow and undertake a modest expansion. Also the real return on money from the lender's point of view is so low in relation to more risky alternatives that people begin to transfer some of their savings into equity investments, which are offering higher potential returns. After a while business activity improves, although the overall level is still not considered to be anywhere near excessive from the point of view of rapidly rising price inflation and interest rates.

Kondratieff observed that at this point there is a tendency for a war to develop, which acts as a catalyst for stronger economic activity. Since there still remains a considerable amount of excess financial and economic capacity, this trough war is not associated with a significant amount of inflation, but as time progresses, each cyclical upwave becomes more pronounced and business once again becomes stronger.

Since price inflation is almost absent, rates of interest are still relatively low and credit is both abundant and cheap. During this early to middle part of the up phase, businesses not only replace old plants and equipment but also invest in new capacity, thereby improving productivity and creating wealth.

This up phase is usually associated with some new technological development, such as canals in the 1820s and 1830s, railroads in the mid-nineteenth century, automobiles in the early part of the twentieth century, and electronics in the 1960s.

As the cycle develops, the hard times are gradually forgotten as each recession turns out to be relatively mild compared with the generally predicted new depression. Confidence, given our natural ability to overextend ourselves, becomes overconfidence. Distortions from overinvestment begin to develop in the economy, leading to social tensions and economic instability. A common characteristic around this peak period is another war, which accentuates these distortions. This was true of the peaks of 1812, 1861, and 1914. Given the fact that business conditions are very strong, this period is naturally associated with very high interest rates and price inflation, often terminating in a runaway commodity bull market.

The plateau period is one of transition or adjustment from the highly emotional and volatile conditions of the peak to that of the deflationary phase. Since interest rates have already reached their secular peaks, the big opportunities for making money from the long side in good-quality bonds occurs during the plateau period, although prices do not usually begin to accelerate on the up side until the down phase of the long wave has begun.

The plateau period is heralded by a collapse in prices and a recession.

The recession in 1920–1921 for example was extremely deep and gave considerable cause for concern. Most businesses quickly recover and do very well during the remaining part of the plateau phase, but many others barely manage to keep ahead, the adjustment in prices from the peak period being too much for them to absorb, often because they were overinvested or excessively leveraged in the previous phase. The agricultural and shipping sectors in the 1920s are prime examples of this. Since the economic recoveries during the plateau period lack the broad strength of earlier years, the reported economic statistics mask the underlying deterioration taking place.

During the plateau period there is usually a swing to the right politically as a result of the volatility and uncertainty of the terminal phase of the upswing. Consequently the budget is usually in a surplus position as pressure is applied to cut government spending and deficits. This is critical since its effect is very deflationary on an economic and financial system that is already vulnerable. While the government budget surplus position is good for the financial position of bondholders since the authorities are actually paying off loans rather than borrowing, other people are not so fortunate since this process sets off the deflationary cycle, which then begins to feed on itself. Eventually another recession sets in, triggering major bankruptcies and causing the economy to fall into the depressionary phase of the cycle. This downwave usually takes several business cycles to work its way out. While it is a good period from the point of view of falling interest rates, credit risk is at its highest. Consequently it is important for investors to concentrate investments in only the highest-quality debt instruments since the threat of actual default in such trying and difficult times is very real.

THE RELEVANCE OF KONDRATIEFF TODAY

In recent years the Kondratieff theory has gained a considerable following, especially among stock market investors. This is because the 1972–1974 commodity boom and Vietnam war, which followed a long period of rising interest rates, appeared to accommodate the predictions the theory called for. A purely mechanistic approach to the theory should be used with extreme caution, however for these reasons:

1. Only three cycles have been observed, which is hardly significant for statistical purposes.

2. It is quite possible that the peak and trough wars occurred quite accidentally and had little connection with the prevailing economic conditions.

3. The role of the government in the economy has increased substantially in the postwar period. While this expanded role has provided a cushion for the economy during recessionary periods, it has also prevented a correction of the excesses of the previous recovery from taking place. As a result productivity has suffered and price inflation has become far more entrenched in the system than before. In addition to government action, other factors such as wage indexing, pension plans, and the like have also acted to prevent the rate of price inflation from coming down during periods when business has been contracting.

4. One of the characteristics associated with the plateau period was a transfer of the government budget position from one of deficit at the termination of the peak period to one of surplus during the years of stability before the down phase. The situation in the late 1970s, when plateau conditions should have been experienced, was quite different, with the United States government running close to a record deficit.

These criticisms are not designed to destroy the theory but merely to caution readers against a mechanistic extrapolation. The truth probably lies somewhere in between. In other words, the Kondratieff wave can be used as a framework from which to work, but since the makeup of political, social, and economic conditions varies from wave to wave, the outcome will also be different.

There is little doubt that there are long-term secular trends in economic activity, but these trends should probably be thought of as inflationary and deflationary *forces* rather than being measured in terms of actual prices. The late 1970s can be considered in this context. Following the sharp global recession of 1974–1975 an economic recovery took place but at the expense of record budget deficits around the world, not only in terms of actual money but in relation to global GNP. Monetary stimulation was also considerable during this period. Stimulation on such a massive scale was necessary to counteract the deflationary forces that were a legacy of the postwar period. What were these deflationary forces and how did they arise?

First, the long period of monetary and fiscal stimulation and the resultant price boom pushed resources into areas that would not be economically justified under periods of price stability. Given the fact that the function of a recession is to correct such pockets of disequilibrium and that the recessions of the later postwar period were prevented from achieving this task, each recovery began with more and more human and physical resources performing uneconomic functions. The burden therefore became that much greater for the productive elements and required greater stimulation to keep the unproductive sectors afloat until the recovery could gain a hold.

Second, the tremendous debts of governments, individuals, and corporations that had accumulated in the postwar period not only had to be serviced but serviced at historically high rates of interest, thereby acting as a drag on the recovery until such debts could be partially erased by price inflation. The huge accumulation of debt that occurred in the 1960s and 1970s could also be looked at as an artificial stimulant to demand since many businesses had made expansionary investment decisions based on this growth in credit. A failure by the authorities to stimulate the economy aggressively and keep the game going would have resulted in a considerable number of self-feeding bankruptcies.

These deflationary forces would therefore have resulted in an even greater recession than occurred in 1974 to 1977, and a significant adjustment would have developed on the price front but for the massive monetary and fiscal stimulation by the United States and other authorities as they sought to avoid a repetition of the extreme political pain of the 1930s.

This discussion may appear at first to be leading away from the subject of interest-rate forecasting. However, it is the position of the secular trend that is so important in helping determine the magnitude and duration that can be expected from a typical 4-year interest-rate cycle. Therefore if the Kondratieff theory is regarded as one of inflationary and deflationary forces, as opposed to rising and falling prices, it still appears to be operating since deflationary forces are operating at a time when they should be.

The longer governments fight this deflationary tide and do not allow the global economy to correct the excesses of the postwar period the greater will be the need for monetary and fiscal stimulation to offset the growing effects of the deflationary forces and the more unlikely we are to see a secular bull market in bonds develop in the 1980s.

Moreover, the longer this process continues the greater will be the tendency for the rate of price inflation to continue expanding in each succeeding business cycle, bringing with it higher and higher interest rates. It is therefore of crucial importance when analyzing the cyclical course of interest rates to evaluate the possibilities for a break in this secular trend as well; for if this were to take place, an extremely significant reversal of the postwar trend of rising interest rates would occur.

6

INTEREST RATES AND THE FEDERAL RESERVE

As already discussed, the price of money, that is, an interest rate, is determined by the interaction of its supply-demand relationship. This chapter outlines the activities of the Federal Reserve and is essentially concerned with the supply part of this equation.

The Federal Reserve cannot force other sectors of the economy to demand credit, but since it has an immense influence over the supply of credit or the conditions relating to its supply, the importance of Federal Reserve policy on the level of interest rates is considerable.

It is not surprising therefore that the game of "Fed watching" has become extremely popular in the investment community, not only in the sense of analyzing the action of the Fed in the markets but also by closely following every word and nuance of Federal Reserve officials for an inkling of what the authorities are thinking and what action they might take.

As will be discussed later, it is the actions of the Fed, which are usually controlled by economic events, that are important to monitor. Speeches and interviews by officials can be very seductive but usually shed little light on what is actually going on and may, in fact, be misleading since the remarks are often politically oriented. Consequently the process of forecasting interest rates is better served by understanding how the Fed operates and what kind of economic and financial developments influence its decisions.

This chapter is concerned with a very simple explanation of some of the techniques of Federal Reserve operations, and the next chapter deals with the economic and financial conditions that are largely responsible for the formulation of monetary policy. Readers who are interested in obtaining the data discussed in this and subsequent chapters should refer to the Appendix, where some of the more important sources are listed.

THE PROCESS OF MONEY CREATION

THE MONETARY BASE

Money creation takes place in the banking system, but the ability of the banks to actually create money is determined by the raw material that the authorities choose to give them. This raw material, known as the *monetary base,* consists of currency in circulation and deposits held by member banks at the Federal Reserve.

For the present, the monetary base may be thought of as a seed, which in turn produces more seed, so that the monetary authorities are able to influence the money supply by raising or lowering the monetary base. Of course the actual number of seeds produced from a harvest will depend not only on the number planted but also on soil and weather conditions. The same is true of the monetary system: the greater the quantity of the monetary base the greater the potential of the financial system to put money in the hands of the public.

Just as the harvest will depend on soil and climatic conditions, so the creation of money from the monetary base, other things being equal, will be a function of prevailing economic and financial conditions.

THE MONEY SUPPLY

Before considering this process of money creation, it is worth obtaining a better understanding of what the money supply actually is. Money has been defined as having three attributes: it is (1) a medium of exchange, (2) a store of value, and (3) a unit of account.

It could be argued that under this definition there is no perfect form of money today since although each of the world's currencies has lost its value to price inflation, gold, which has retained its value, is not widely accepted as a medium of exchange or a unit of account.

It is little wonder therefore that the authorities, whose definitions are limited to that of a paper currency, have many different definitions of the money supply. Some people, for example, prefer to regard actual currency in circulation and demand deposits (that is, non-interest-bearing deposits on which a check can be drawn) as the money supply. This definition, known as M_{1A}, is a narrow definition of money supply. On the other hand some economists prefer to add other checkable deposits at banks and thrift institutions since they say quite rightly that it is an easy process to convert savings deposits into cash. This definition is known as M_{1B}. The definition of money can be expanded still further to include certificates of deposit, thrift institution deposits, money market funds, and bank noncheckable deposits. These broader money-supply definitions are shown in Table 6-1.

THE BANKING SYSTEM

The actual creation of money takes place in the banking system. Banks are essentially wholesalers of money in that they accept deposits from some customers at a specific interest rate (or in the case of demand deposits no interest at all) and lend it out to others at a higher rate, the difference representing the banks' gross profit. While other wholesalers are limited to selling the goods they purchase, the banking system can, if it chooses, "sell" more loans than the deposits taken in. Naturally banks are keen to make as many creditworthy loans as they can since this will increase their profitability. However, they are required to put a certain percentage of their deposits on a non-interest-bearing basis with the Federal Reserve. The actual proportion varies according to the prevailing monetary policy of the authorities. There are also different requirements for different types of deposits. Because of their relative stability, time deposits, for example,

TABLE 6-1 Different Definitions of Money

M_{1A}	M_{1B}	M_2	M_3
Currency plus demand deposits	M_{1A} plus other checkable deposits at banks and thrift institutions	M_{1B} plus overnight repurchase agreements and Eurodollars, money market mutual fund shares, and savings and small time deposits at commercial banks and thrift institutions	M_2 plus large time deposits and term repurchase agreements at commercial banks and thrift institutions

are faced with lower reserve requirements than demand deposits, which can be withdrawn at any time. It is only when a bank has reserves in excess of its required amount that it is able to create money.

It does so in the following way. The assets of a bank can be divided into loans, which account for the greatest proportion, and investments, of which government securities are the largest part. If the Federal Reserve decides to buy $1000 of government securities from a securities dealer, it gives the dealer a check drawn on the Federal Reserve Bank. When the dealer deposits the check, this automatically increases the bank's cash reserves at the Federal Reserve, as reserves are bank deposits held at the Fed. In view of the fact that such deposits do not earn interest, it is to the bank's advantage to loan out or invest most of the $1000, the remainder being kept as the required reserves. If the prevailing reserve requirement was 20 percent, this would split the $1000 into $200 held as reserve and $800 to be loaned. If the bank decides to loan out the money, the amount will be credited to the borrower's account, thereby increasing the money supply by $800. The borrower will probably spend the money, which will subsequently be credited as a deposit in the recipients' accounts at other banks, of which a proportion will be soaked up as reserves at the Fed and the remainder loaned out or invested. This secondary effect will also result in an increase in the money supply to the tune of $640 (20 percent of $800; $160 deposited as reserves and $640 loaned out or invested) and so on.

Whether this money is loaned or invested is important from the point of view of the future course of interest rates, but from the point of view of money creation either use of reserves by banks creates money. For example, during a recession when the authorities are attempting to promote a policy of monetary ease, the demand for credit is generally low. Since banks wish to make the best use of government-supplied money, the tendency is for them to purchase government or other securities from private holders rather than create loans (or hold non-interest-bearing excess reserves). The cash that the sellers of these debt instruments receive is then deposited at their bank branches, with the same multiplier ramifications as for the proceeds from a newly created loan. However, the banks' purchase of securities has the effect of increasing demand for securities, thereby pushing up prices and pulling interest rates down.

At a later stage in the cycle when business activity begins to pick up, not only will the banks be more willing to create loans (since the risk of default will have shrunk) but corporations and individuals themselves will actually be demanding credit. As a result, any further injection of reserves into the system will tend to be used by the banks more for loan creation than for security acquisition. Also banks themselves will be actively bidding for wholesale deposits such as CDs to finance this large and growing demand for credit in the private sector.

When loan growth begins to outstrip the increase in deposits, interest rates will start to rise. It is therefore important to distinguish between the supply-induced increase in money supply resulting from security purchases and the demand-induced growth emanating from expanding credit demands. This topic is discussed at greater length in Chapter 8.

The twofold key to the whole money-creating process is, first, the willingness of the authorities to increase the monetary base through either the purchase of securities (as described above), known as *open-market operations,* or a change in the rules that would lower the amount of reserves required by the Federal Reserve. This latter technique, if adopted, has the effect of freeing up some of the reserves held by the various banks for lending or investing.* Second is the willingness of the banking system and/or the public to use these excess reserves, in the sense that the banks wish to lend or invest any of their surplus deposits and the private sector is willing to take on more loans.

THE FEDERAL FUNDS AND DISCOUNT RATES

At any given time, some banks will have an excess of reserves and others will have a deficiency. It is possible for a deficient bank to borrow overnight from a surplus one and use the borrowed reserves to make up the deficiency in its requirement. The interest rate charged for this transaction, known as the *federal funds rate,* is determined by the supply-demand relationship of required reserves between the various banks. Since the Federal Reserve can influence the total supply of reserves outstanding by buying and selling securities for its own account, it is able to control the level of the federal funds rate. It is therefore important to monitor this key interest rate since its trend often gives a clue to the direction of monetary policy.

When the banking system as a whole is deficient in its reserve requirements, it does have one option, namely, to borrow some reserves from the Federal Reserve. The interest rate paid is known as the *discount rate.* If the Federal Reserve considers that the banks are using this facility excessively, it discourages them from doing so by raising the discount rate, because borrowing at the discount window is only intended to help banks in an

---

*On the other hand, raising the reserve requirement or the sale of securities by the Federal Reserve would have the effect of *reducing* the amount of free reserves in the system.

emergency situation, not as a source of cheap money from which to generate greater profits. While the federal funds rate fluctuates from day to day, changes in the discount rate are made infrequently and denote either a shift or reversal in monetary policy. Because both the federal funds rate and the discount rate affect the cost of borrowed money for the banking system, they have a significant impact on the level of other short-term interest rates.

In view of this influence, the monetary authorities do not make decisions on changes in the discount rate lightly, just as boards of corporate directors consider changes in dividend policies very carefully. If the Federal Reserve were to change its policies regularly, it would lead to confusion and a loss of confidence by the financial community. Consequently if following a series of discount rate hikes over a 12- to 24-month period the authorities alter course and *reduce* the discount rate, this can usually be taken as a very strong sign that monetary policy has reversed from one of stringency to one of ease. Normally at this point short-term rates will already have reached their peak and begun to turn down. The reverse situation is also true in that the first hike in the discount rate following many months of decline will indicate that the Federal Reserve is taking a more cautious stance. It should be noted that in most cases the discount rate follows other short-term interest rates instead of leading them.

Charts 6-1 and 6-2 show the discount rate and the prime rate with several other short-term interest rates. They point up the close relationship between the administered (discount rate) and free market rates. Normally the Federal Reserve begins to ease up when it senses that the previous period of monetary tightening has had its required effect on cooling the economy. Most of the time this judgment proves to be correct, and it can be assumed that interest rates are then in for a cyclical decline. Occasionally, as in August 1968, the Fed's decision to lower the discount rate can be premature. In that case it was forced to reverse its policy in December and continue a policy of tight money for the next year. This period has been cited as an example showing that no one indicator can be used consistently to signal when a cyclical reversal in interest rates has taken place. The discussion in Chapter 9, for example, which focuses on some key economic indicators, will demonstrate that the economy was not weak enough to be consistent with an interest-rate peak. This example serves as a fine warning that all the various factors going into the supply-demand aspect of interest rates should be considered before reaching a firm conclusion about their future cyclical course.

An example of the opposite type developed in the spring of 1974. This

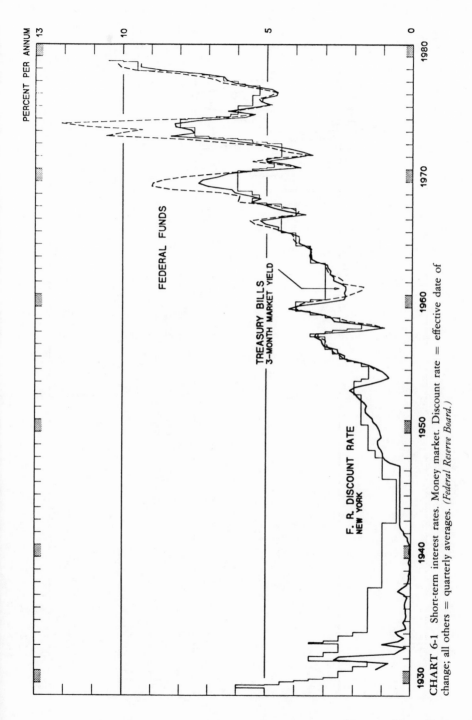

CHART 6-1 Short-term interest rates. Money market. Discount rate = effective date of change; all others = quarterly averages. *(Federal Reserve Board.)*

75

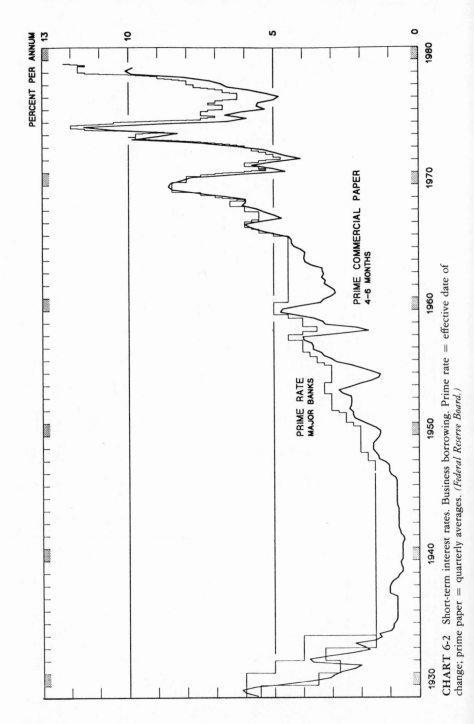

PRIME RATE
MAJOR BANKS

PRIME COMMERCIAL PAPER
4–6 MONTHS

CHART 6-2 Short-term interest rates. Business borrowing. Prime rate = effective date of change; prime paper = quarterly averages. *(Federal Reserve Board.)*

period was preceded by a declining economy as measured by many of the leading economic indicators, a drying up in the growth of credit demands, and sharply falling short-term interest rates. In other words, everything looked set for a cyclical interest-rate peak. However, at no point in the January to March period was the discount rate lowered. In fact the drop did not come until December of that year. Although this occurred well after the late summer peak in short-term interest rates, it was fairly close to the October low in bond prices and early enough to permit a sound investment policy to be set for the ensuing cycle. On the other hand, it would have been extremely expensive, especially at the long end of the debt market, to have jumped the gun in February or March of 1974 purely on the basis of a weakening economy.

THE FEDERAL RESERVE AND CONTROL OF THE MONEY SUPPLY

In recent years the popularity of monetary economics has encouraged many central banks, including the Federal Reserve, to announce official targets for money-supply growth. As discussed earlier, growth of the money supply is largely a function of the ability and willingness of the banking system to create credit. It therefore follows that the central bank can only take indirect measures to control money growth. After all, if the Federal Reserve puts a substantial amount of reserves into the system and the banks are unwilling to expand loans or purchase investments, the money supply will not grow.

It is one thing for the Federal Reserve to set money-supply goals and another to achieve them. The actual economic implications of achieving such goals are also disputable. As discussed earlier, it is very difficult to define an appropriate measure of money, because of both conceptual problems and institutional changes, which in turn influence the various monetary measures. A 10 percent growth for M_2 in one business cycle may have a completely different effect from another where institutional developments such as money market funds; NOW accounts, and the like, affect the way the public chooses to hold its cash balances.

The process of controlling the level of business activity through money-supply growth is clearly fraught with many pitfalls and is by no means as simple as first appears, but from the point of view of forecasting interest rates it is important for investors to monitor the level of money growth in relation to the stated targets in order to assess whether government policy is likely to be more restrictive or less. For example, if the money-growth target of M_2 has been rising at a 10 percent rate over the previous 6 months compared with a government target of 6 percent, and assuming that the target will remain unchanged, you can be fairly sure that monetary policy will have to become more restrictive in order to bring the money-supply growth down to its target level. This restraining process would of course result in higher interest rates as the Fed drains reserves from the banking system.

The relationship between targeted and actual monetary growth rates is widely covered in the financial press, and that is probably the best place for investors to monitor such developments.

If investors choose to follow this relationship on their own, it is important to average out the money-supply figures over many weeks because the weekly figures themselves can be greatly distorted by erroneous seasonal adjustments, reporting problems, and so on. To base conclusions on 1 week's figures can be potentially disastrous.

7
UNDERSTANDING FEDERAL RESERVE POLICIES

One of the best ways to try to come to grips with Federal Reserve policies, both current and future, is to put yourself in the position of the authorities and consider how you would act if you were running the nation's monetary policy. Bear in mind that the Federal Reserve was originally formed to create monetary policies that would help to protect the economy from the sharp fluctuations that had previously occurred.

Essentially the Federal Reserve walks the cyclical tightrope between the control of inflation on one hand and the prevention of unemployment on the other. Although in theory the Fed is completely independent of the elected representatives of the people, in practice it is not; for while the Federal Reserve chairman and the board of governors are appointed and hold office long enough to span several elections, they are still subject to political pressures. Since the board does not have a mandate from the electorate, any serious deviation from what would be generally accepted as prudent action would undoubtedly result in quick legislative action by Congress. For example, if the board considered that excessive inflationary pressures were building up before a major election and adopted an extremely tight monetary policy, strong political pressure would be mounted for the chairman and the board to reverse their stance and perhaps even be removed from office. For this reason it is normally safe to assume that while the Fed will usually adopt a more conservative policy than the politicians would like, the political pressure, actual or potential, will stop them from becoming as conservative as events might justify.

A brief explanation of the interaction of monetary growth with economic activity will help to elucidate the Fed's dilemma. Figure 7-1 also

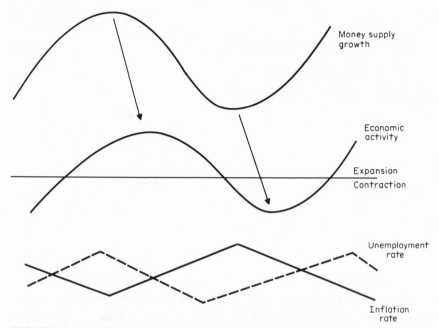

FIGURE 7-1   *(top)* The lead characteristic of monetary growth over economic activity. *(bottom)* The relationship between the rate of price inflation and the unemployment rate. After a lag the Fed stimulates business activity by encouraging a growth in monetary expansion. While expanding economic activity brings the unemployment level down, it also puts upward pressure on the inflation rate, so that there is a continual trade-off between them during the course of the business cycle. The most comfortable period for the authorities develops just after the economy begins to expand, since the inflation rate is low and relatively stable and unemployment has started to come down. Conversely, the most difficult period is just before the recession, when the inflation rate appears to be getting out of control and unemployment has also started to rise.

shows this relationship in graphic form. Even though monetary growth rates have peaked and the rate of business activity has begun to slow at the end of the business cycle, price inflation rates continue to expand and so the Fed adopts a tight money policy. This deflates the level of economic activity into negative territory and results in an expansion of the unemployment rate. Realizing that it has overreacted, the Fed reverses its monetary policy to one of ease by lowering reserve requirements and pumping reserves into the system. Banks respond by using these additional reserves to increase their investments, mainly in the form of purchase of government securities, which in turn reverses the downward trend of monetary growth. Given this increased demand for debt securities combined with the continuing decrease in loan demand due to the recession, interest rates fall dramatically during this period. In a sense price inflation is being transferred from the real economy to the financial economy as bond and stock prices respond favorably to the lower interest rates.

At some point the excesses of the previous recovery, such as surplus inventory and overmanning, are corrected; and since money is easier to obtain than in the period of credit tightening and also much cheaper due to the decline in interest rates, businesses and consumers begin to expand their levels of activity and a new recovery is under way. Since inflationary pressures are still moderating and unemployment is at a high level, the Fed continues to feel comfortable about a maintained policy of monetary ease.

At some point, however, the increase in the money supply begins to have a more robust effect on the level of business activity as unemployment falls off, price inflation begins to pick up, and short-term interest rates start to surge upward. At this point the Fed is faced with the prospect of reining in some of the monetary expansion, but since the situation appears to be well under control, little action is usually taken, especially as such inaction is well received by the politicians. This was the case, for example, in mid-1971. Then the consumer price inflation rate had fallen from just under 7 to 4 percent, but unemployment, which is very much a lagging indicator of the economy, was still around what was considered at that time to be an uncomfortable level of 6 percent. Given the lags between monetary expansion and contraction and changes in the level of economic activity, there was no scope for monetary contraction and restimulation before the 1972 election, so that the political pressures were all in the direction of continued stimulation, which was what in fact occurred.

The 1973–1974 experience was typical of the next phase in the cycle, where the previously created money moves out of the financial markets (which continue deflating in price) into the real economy as business activity picks up substantial momentum. As inflation reaches unacceptably high levels, the Fed again returns to a tight money policy by restricting the expansion of credit. At this point the economy has usually begun to weaken anyway, so that the measures prove to be those of overkill, sending the economy into an even sharper recession.

Even though the Fed is forced into a tight money policy when inflationary pressures get out of hand, this does not mean that it does not take any restrictive action up to this point. The problem is that the authorities usually lean on the side of insufficient restraint, preferring to keep interest rates down by pumping reserves into the system. As the cycle progresses, this excessive monetary growth translates into greater economic momentum and higher rates of price inflation. This in turn leads to a rapid expansion of credit demands and even higher interest rates, until eventually the Fed is forced into administering the strong medicine it should have given earlier.

Apart from the domestic discipline put on the Fed by the financial markets, excessive monetary creation also feeds back in the form of external pressures. For example, because of the stimulative effect of money on the economy, a country experiencing excessive monetary growth relative to its trading partners will tend to import a higher volume of goods than its competitors. Also its manufacturing industries will tend to produce more goods for the booming domestic economy than for exports. These factors will affect the balance of payments adversely and will cause downward pressure on the inflating country's currency, again forcing the central bank to rein in the excessive growth of money. This type of situation caused a run on the American dollar between 1977 and 1978, resulting in the so-called Carter package. A similar currency crisis was halted by belated central bank action in the United Kingdom in October 1976.

Another example of enforced discipline can occur if strong economic momentum pushes up credit demands and then interest rates. If the Fed does not follow through with a discount-rate hike, banks will turn to the discount window since the discount rate, that is, the rate banks pay for borrowing reserves, will represent a bargain and they will borrow all they can at this rate. If this process is allowed to continue too far, the money supply will balloon, so eventually of course the Fed is forced to take some restrictive action.

Generally speaking, the longer the Fed avoids painful action the higher the ultimate cyclical peak in interest rates will be. One should never assume that because the governors of the Federal Reserve are learned and experienced people backed by a wealth of staff support they will usually make the correct decisions. Nothing could be farther from the truth. After all, if the authorities really knew what they were doing, it is highly unlikely that they would have permitted the astronomical interest and inflation rates of the 1970s and early 1980s. The problem is that many decisions are subject to committees, compromise, political pressure, and an underestimation of inflationary pressures. Furthermore, over a long period of time significant institutional changes take place because of alterations in banking regulations and the behavior of the public due to changes in the financial environment. For example, the sharp increase in interest rates in the 1970s gave rise to the development of money market funds, automatic transfer accounts, bank repurchase agreements, and so on, which were essentially designed as vehicles for individuals and corporations with cash to obtain high interest rates. Since these liquid assets were until recently excluded from money-supply definitions, the effect was to understate the growth of money balances using the traditional M_1 and M_2 measures of money. But since this liquidity was still in the system, the Federal Reserve, with its badly distorted data, was clearly not in a position to make the correct decisions.

Another factor has been the change in regulation Q interest-rate ceilings. Under this regulation many financial institutions have been forbidden by law to pay over a certain amount in interest rates on certain classes of deposits. For example, up to 1969 it was illegal for banks to pay more than 5 percent on certificates of deposit. Over the years the restraints of regulation Q, combined with many state usury laws, have been eased, so that it is possible for the system to support higher interest rates before recessionary conditions set in. Given such complex changes and the difficulty of assessing their impact on the economy, it is little wonder that the central bank has erred in its judgment of the appropriate level of monetary expansion and interest rates.

CROWDING OUT

The expression "crowding out," which appears frequently in the financial press, is often used in an incorrect or misleading context. Crowding out refers to the competition for borrowed funds between the federal government and the private sector when there are insufficient savings in the system to satisfy them both. Since the government is relatively insensitive to the rate of interest it has to pay, private borrowers are in a sense crowded out of the market. There is a limit to the rate of interest corporations and individuals can afford to pay to maintain a high level of spending. Thus if the government borrowing requirement is too large in relation to available savings at prevailing levels of interest, the authorities simply raise rates to the level required to sell the debt so that other potential borrowers are unable to obtain their financing. The phenomenon of crowding out essentially occurs at a late stage in the business cycle, when the personal and corporate sectors are experiencing financial difficulties as expenditures expand relative to cash flows. It does not necessarily develop when government borrowing requirements are at their highest since such periods are usually associated with weak economic activity when the private sector is building up cash reserves. At such times the private sector is in a position to accommodate the government since it is a net supplier of funds. Therefore in order to get to the crowding-out stage both the government and the private sector must be running in a deficit position.

Since crowding-out pressures develop from an insufficiency of funds, it is possible for the authorities to avoid a sharp rise in interest rates (at least in the short term) by injecting deposits into the system. In effect this is done by having the Federal Reserve purchase a significant amount of the newly issued government debt, thereby putting deposits into the banking system. Between 1955 and 1965, for example, federal budget deficits resulted in the creation of $31 billion new debt, of which the Fed acquired 50 percent. This money is then lent or invested by the banks, thereby creating more money and so on. In the 1955–1965 decade, when deficits were small, money supply M_1 grew at a moderate 2.2 percent average annual rate, consumer prices rose 1.7 percent per annum on average, while yields on AAA corporate bonds averaged about 4 percent. During the following 10 years, 1965–1975, aggregate federal deficits resulted in the issuing of $141 billion new federal debt, of which the Fed purchased a third. However, money growth, inflation, and bond yields rose to 5.5, 5.4, and 6.9 percent, respectively during this period.

Given the development of crowding-out pressures, the authorities are therefore left with the choice of printing money or drawing on the available cash balances of the private sector. The first alternative will inflate the money supply and delay the rise in interest rates; the second will result in an immediate short but sharp rise in interest rates. In practice the authorities usually compromise by allowing interest rates to rise a little by financing part of the deficit through monetary creation. Inevitably, this ultimately results in an acceleration of the rate of price inflation which encourages an even higher level of private borrowing. This leads to additional financial pressures and an eventual economic downturn. The recession greatly reduces private-sector borrowing to the extent that this sector begins a liquidity-building program, so that it becomes a net supplier of funds. In 1976, for example, when the economic recovery was at a relatively early stage, the government borrowing requirement, as a result of the budget deficit, was at a new record level of about $66 billion, but since the private sector was relatively liquid, it was only necessary for the Federal Reserve to purchase about 10 percent of the newly created debt. In fact the private sector was so flush with funds that rates actually fell on balance during that year.

In conclusion, when assessing the possibility of crowding-out pressures, readers should first pay close attention to the current position of the business cycle to establish the financial position of the private sector and then make an assessment of how the deficit is going to be financed— through credit creation or by drawing on existing funds in the system.

It seems evident from the above discussion that you should always try to put yourself in the position of the Federal Reserve Board, from the point of view both of their assessment of the prevailing economic situation and issues and of potential political pressures, remembering that when in doubt the central bank will usually adopt a policy of ease rather than restraint. Only when inflation rates become unacceptable do the authorities take the necessary and painful action.

This is not to imply that the central bank will never adopt an appropriate policy of restraint at the early stages of the business cycle, but since the record of the U.S. Federal Reserve and other central banks has almost universally been of the inappropriate inflationary type, it seems unlikely that less pragmatic short-term policies will continue to be adopted in the future.

8
INTEREST RATES
AND LIQUIDITY

The discussion in Chapter 7 concerning the operations of the Federal Reserve has prepared the ground for an exploration of the effect of changes in liquidity on the trend of interest rates.

Liquidity has been defined as the ability to meet demand for a payment. It is essentially a very subjective concept since what might be a comfortable level of liquidity for one entity under any given circumstance might not be suitable for another. In other words, if two people have a $10,000 deposit in a bank account and both suffer an unexpected financial setback which costs each of them $5000, one person may feel it necessary to save enough money to bring the balance back to the $10,000 while the other, still regretting the setback, may choose to leave the balance at $5000. Aggregated for the whole financial system, the level and changes in liquid assets have a tremendous effect on the economy, inflation, and interest rates.

For forecasting interest rates, liquidity is important from two points of view: (1) the overall level of liquidity, that is, the amount of surplus liquid assets in the system, and (2) the rate of change of liquidity. Before distinguishing between these two concepts, it is worth discussing how liquidity can be measured.

The most useful liquidity data come from the banking system; for not only does the banking system provide the financial framework on which the rest of the economy is based, but the data are also very timely and are usually reported 2 to 3 weeks after the fact. This is very important since many economic and financial data are reported with a lag up to 2 to 4 months. While a really up-to-date picture is not always necessary, relatively current statistics are required around major cyclical turning points so that a reversal can be identified sooner and more easily. A further advantage of banking data, is that they are relatively accurate and can therefore be used for forecasting purposes. Finally, banking data, in their broadest form, are available right back to the pre-1920 era, making it possible to construct indicators developed from banking data that compare interest-rate and liquidity trends going back over a substantial number of business cycles. One caveat is needed, however; the half century or so for which the data are available has been subject to several institutional changes, which would distort the indicators if they were not properly adjusted. For this reason it is important to understand the conceptual design of these indicators and to make adjustments as and when any further institutional changes take place. If such adjustments are not made, the various indicators will give a misleading impression of what is actually going on in the banking system.

Essentially these liquidity indicators should measure the relationship between the demand for money and its supply. In the banking system the demand for money is reflected by the trend of loan growth; the supply is measured by fluctuations in bank deposits. If loans are expanding at a faster rate than deposits, this means that the demand for money is outstripping its supply, resulting in an increase in the price of money, that is, interest rates. A change in this relationship in favor of deposits will obviously have the reverse effect and result in falling interest rates and rising bond prices. Several other ways of measuring banking liquidity will be discussed later, but now it is appropriate to discuss the significance of the overall level of liquidity in the system compared with changes in that level.

DISTINGUISHING BETWEEN THE ABSOLUTE LEVEL OF LIQUIDITY AND RELATIVE CHANGES IN THE LEVEL OF LIQUIDITY

The discussion in Chapter 5 showed that there are two important forces working on the level of interest rates: the secular, or long-term, trend and the business-cycle, or shorter-term, trend. The absolute level of liquidity appears to be the dominant force affecting the level of interest rates at any particular time, while the rate of change in liquidity is an important force affecting the trend of interest rates. Since the level of interest rates changes substantially during the course of the business cycle, the rate of change of liquidity is useful for forecasting cyclical changes in interest rates. On the other hand, since the long-term changes in the absolute level of liquidity affect the actual level of interest rates at any particular time, an observation of liquidity levels is useful from the point of view of identifying secular movements in interest rates. Chart 8-1 shows the long-term relationship between a measure of banking liquidity and long-term interest rates.

Chart 8-2 shows various liquidity measures compared with Moody's Aaa Corporate Bond Yield during the postwar period. The bond-yield index has been plotted inversely to correspond with bond prices and to emphasize the deterioration in liquidity during this period. The first series monitors the changes in liquidity of corporations. It is a ratio of cash assets as a percentage of current liabilities of United States corporations. Cash assets are defined as cash and money market securities, while current liabilities are obligations that corporations are expected to meet in the next 12 months. Because of revisions in the data, three different measures of this series have been reported during this period and account for the two breaks in the series during the 1960s. The various series have therefore been overlapped for comparative purposes.

The chart shows quite clearly that corporate liquidity as defined by this particular ratio (do not forget there are many ways of measuring corporate

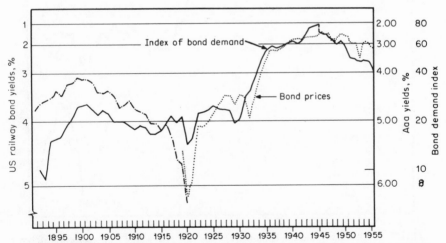

CHART 8-1   The background of the bond market. The Index of bond demand means adjusted deposits less loans and discounts for all banks in the United States as of 30 June, 1892 to 1945, as a percentage of adjusted deposits and thereafter Federal Reserve Member Banks quarterly, 1946 to date. Data from *Historical Statistics of the United States, 1879–1945, Survey of Current Business*, and *Federal Reserve Bulletins*. Bond prices are average yearly inverted yields of high-grade railway bonds, 1891 to 1920. Moody's Aaa corporate inverted yields 1919 to 1955. Data from *Historical Statistics, Federal Reserve Banking and Monetary Statistics, Survey of Current Business*, and *Federal Reserve Bulletins*. *(The Bank Credit Analyst.)*

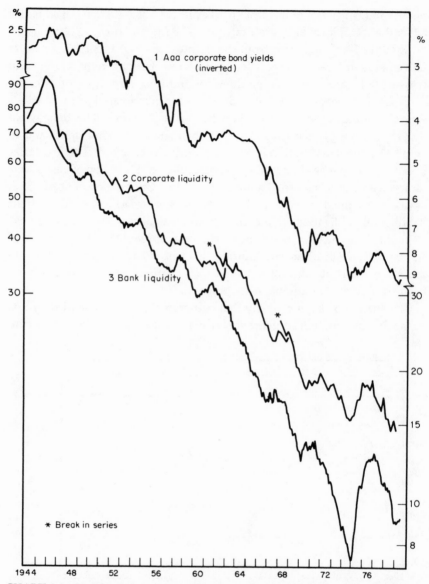

CHART 8-2 Liquidity and the bond market. Curve 1: average of daily figures of Moody's corporate Aaa bonds. Curve 2: cash assets of current liabilities of United States corporations. Curve 3: government securities as a percentage of total commercial bank credit. *(The Bank Credit Analyst.)*

liquidity) has deteriorated in each of the successive postwar business cycles under consideration. Whereas corporations had $80 of cash or near cash to cover every $100 of current liabilities in the mid-1940s, this figure shrank to just under $15 by the late 1970s.

The banking liquidity measure shows a similar trend. This series monitors the amount of government securities held by banks as a percentage of total bank credit. Bank credit consists essentially of bank loans and investments. Investments consist mainly of government securities and state and local government bonds. Government securities form a large part of total bank investments. These instruments are of the very highest quality in terms of credit risk and are also the most easily marketable type of security. If banks run into trouble, they can quickly sell their government securities to raise cash since there is always a ready buyer. On the other hand, loans, which form the vast majority of total bank credit, are far riskier since there is always the chance of default however creditworthy the borrower. Consequently the greater the proportion of bank credit in the form of government securities the more financially sound, or liquid, the banking system will tend to be. This series too is shown in the chart to have been deteriorating throughout the postwar period. The recovery during some business cycles has been nothing less than an upward blip. Whereas 1944 saw government securities forming 70 percent of total bank credit, the ratio slipped as low as 7½ percent in late 1974. These are only two of the many ways in which it is possible to illustrate the long-term decline in liquidity. Other measurements would include the ratio of personal disposable income to debt repayments (Chart 8-3) and total borrowing requirements as a percentage of the GNP.

Charts 8-1 and 8-2 show that there is a very strong correlation between the level of liquidity and that of interest rates. It seems that the more liquidity is run down the higher interest rates become and vice versa. This is because liquidity levels are closely related to inflation, which in turn is closely tied to interest rates. (This latter relationship is discussed in Chapter 10.) The reason is that as inflation increases, individuals and corporations feel more comfortable holding real assets or borrowing money since the declining value of their dollars will reduce the real purchasing value of their liquid assets. On the other hand, if prices are declining or stable, as they were in the 1930s, these same groups choose liquidity and safety over real assets so that liquidity levels rise as price inflation rates fall or actual deflation of prices sets in.

It is therefore little wonder that consumers in the late 1970s, faced with what seemed to be ever-expanding rates of price inflation, chose to mort-

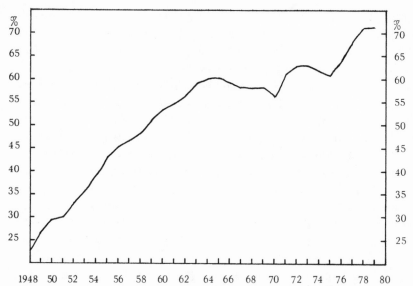

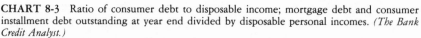

CHART 8-3   Ratio of consumer debt to disposable income; mortgage debt and consumer installment debt outstanding at year end divided by disposable personal incomes. *(The Bank Credit Analyst.)*

gage their houses and resort to other forms of credit, spending the money on real assets or goods in preference to saving it in banks or other financial institutions.

While this long-term decline in liquidity looks extremely serious, as indeed it is, most measurements of liquidity probably exaggerate the deterioration that has actually taken place for two reasons. First, the development of computers and communications technology in the last 30 years has resulted in significant gains in cash-management efficiencies. As a result it is possible for corporations, banks, governments, and individuals to maintain lower cash balances today and meet their payments just as comfortably. In effect these changes have meant that institutions now need far less liquidity than formerly. Second, the forced saving that grew out of World War II meant that liquidity levels were historically and probably unnecessarily high at the beginning of the postwar period, again having the effect of exaggerating the actual deterioration that has taken place since then.

This is not to suggest that the overall level of liquidity had not sunk to a dangerous low by the late 1970s and early 1980s. The record high interest rates and price inflation experienced during this period are a solid testimony that they had. Moreover, these low levels of liquid resources are a prime reason why financial conditions in the last few years have become more volatile and unpredictable and also point up the vulnerability of the financial system as a whole to an unexpected shock.

Obviously corporations or individuals who have run down their cash balances or are even in a net debtor position are far more vulnerable to a general economic downturn or other debilitating shock than those with a strong cash position. When it is considered that the whole financial system is in a weak position, overburdened with debt, it can be appreciated how very little in the way of an adverse development is required to push the system into a serious collapse.

Unfortunately these liquidity series do not indicate an absolute level of liquidity below which the system could no longer function. Nevertheless they do demonstrate quite clearly the strong relationship between levels of liquidity and levels of interest rates.

CYCLICAL CHANGES IN LIQUIDITY

While these longer-term trends are helpful in pointing up the dominant secular forces and therefore useful as background information, it is the *rate of change of liquidity* that must be examined for the purpose of forecasting the cyclical trend of interest rates.

It can be shown that individuals and corporations can adjust to, and live with, new levels of liquidity, interest rates, and inflation rates, but it is the adjustment process itself that is important in the dynamics of the interest-rate cycle since this period is characterized by a rapid change between the balance of the supply of money and the demand for it.

Chart 8-4 shows the dynamics of the interest-rate cycle so far as the supply-demand equation for money is concerned. The top indicator is the rate of growth of M_2, which includes currency, demand, and savings deposits at commercial banks as classified by the Federal Reserve before 1980. The middle indicator is a series representing the rate of growth of bank loans, while the series at the bottom shows the monthly yield on 4- to 6-month commercial paper. The arrows above each series pointing down from left to right are intended to show the chronological development of the dynamics of the interest-rate cycle.

When the money supply and loan series are above their respective horizontal lines at the 100 level, both series are expanding at a rate above their long-term trend. A movement below these lines shows that money supply and/or the total amount of loans outstanding is falling relative to this 8-year trend. Reference to the chart shows that each of the cyclical

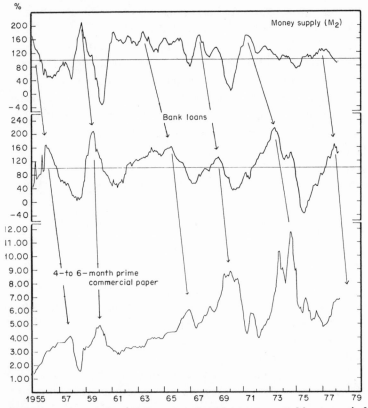

CHART 8-4 Money growth, loan growth, and interest rates. Money supply M_2, 9-month moving average of annualized month-to-month change (ratio to trend). Bank loans (all loans, all banks), 9-month moving average of annualized month-to-month change (ratio to trend). *(Interest Rate Forecast.)*

interest-rate peaks in the 25-year period under consideration was preceded first by a peak in the growth rate of the money supply and then by a peak in the loan growth.

Similarly, interest-rate troughs have a tendency to be preceded by a reversal in the downward trend of both monetary and credit growth. Conceptually, interest-rate troughs are characterized by deposit growth (increases in supply) and loan growth (demand) coming into balance. When loan growth begins to outstrip deposits, interest rates begin to rise. In a sense this point marks a juncture at which the supply-induced (that is, Federal Reserve–induced) growth of the money supply, discussed in the previous chapter, and the demand-induced (that is, economically induced) growth come into balance. When interest rates rise, it is normally a demon-

stration that the influence of loan growth on the money supply is outgrow-
ing the government-induced effect.

The reverse is true at interest-rate peaks where the rate of loan growth
contracts sharply. Even though this has the effect of reducing the overall
growth rate of the money supply, interest rates are able to fall since this
is the point at which recessionary conditions are prevalent and governments begin adopting policies of monetary ease.

Since monetary growth tends to be a passive phenomenon, forecasting
interest rates can be accomplished better by observing trends in the demand for money. In this respect the most sensitive and encompassing
measure for the demand for money is that of loan growth.

Chart 8-5 shows several measures of loan demand expressed on a rate-
of-change basis and compared with the monthly yield of 4- to 6-month
commercial paper. The various series are calculated by dividing one month
by the previous month to obtain the monthly rate change. The result is
then multiplied by 12 to arrive at the rate of change on an annualized basis.
Since this figure is extremely volatile on a month-to-month basis, it is then
smoothed by a 9-month moving average. The statistical technique of constructing moving averages is discussed in Chapter 9.

The resulting index oscillates up and down in response to the cyclical
movement of loan growth, but instead of *lagging* interest-rate peaks and
troughs as the raw data would, loans expressed on a rate-of-change basis
have a tendency to *lead* these important cyclical turning points. In this
respect, the loan series shown at the top, that is, all loans of all commercial
banks and commercial paper, is the most useful. Monthly data on loans can
be obtained from the G. 7 *Statistical Release* of the Federal Reserve, a sample
of which is shown in the Appendix (Table A-I). The data for both loans
and deposits used to calculate the indicators discussed in this chapter have
been seasonally adjusted.

Reference to Chart 8-5 shows that a peak in this index has preceded
every cyclical interest-rate peak in the 25-year period between 1955 and
1980. Consequently it is fairly safe to assume that as long as loan growth
is expanding, interest rates, having reversed their cyclical downtrend, will
continue to rise. While this is useful information to know, it is not particularly helpful from the point of view of timing the peak in interest rates
since the lead time between the peak in loan growth and that of interest
rates varies considerably from cycle to cycle. One method that can improve
the timing is to compare the 9-month moving average of the monthly rate
of change of loan growth to a 96-month moving average. The 96-month

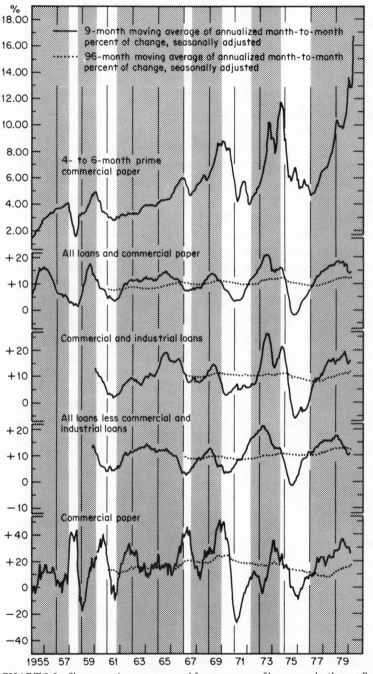

CHART 8-5   Short-term interest rates and four measures of loan growth. *(Interest Rate Forecast.)*

(8-year) moving average is represented on Chart 8-5 by the dashed line. It seems that when the 9-month moving average of loan growth has contracted sufficiently to cross below its 96-month counterpart, the peak in interest rates has either occurred or is just about to occur. The record of this approach is far from perfect, but the use of the 96-month moving average, which in effect smooths away the distortions of two (4-year) business cycles, greatly improves the timing.

The relationship between loan growth and interest rates is less precise at interest-rate lows. For example, the interest-rate troughs of 1961 and 1966 more or less coincided with a trough in loan growth while that of 1958 actually led the loan series. Only at the 1972 and 1976 interest-rate bottoms did loan growth actually precede the low in interest rates by a significant margin. Quite clearly an analysis of loan growth, while helpful, is not quite so useful when the cyclical trend of interest rates is about to reverse from down to up, as at interest-rate peaks.

Since loan demand represents only one-half of the supply-demand relationship of money, it is important to measure the interraction of both sides. This relationship is represented in Chart 8-6. The top of the chart is an absolute measure of the relationship between loans* (demand) and deposits† (supply) derived from the following formula:

$$(\text{deposits} - \text{loans}) \div \text{deposits}$$

Below this series is that of the yield on Moody's Aaa bonds, which again have been plotted inversely to correspond to bond prices. Reference to the chart shows that the liquidity and bond-yield series move relatively closely together. However, during 1963 to 1965 yields were basically unchanged while the liquidity series deteriorated gradually. In other words, since the speed of the financial deterioration was not particularly strong, interest rates were relatively unaffected because people could adjust to these slow changes in liquidity levels. Eventually, at the beginning of 1965, the liquidity series began to fall sharply, to be followed later in the year by an equally sharp fall in bond prices, that is, rise in yields.

This example shows that it is the *speed* at which liquidity levels adjust that is important in putting upward or downward pressure on interest-rate movements, but it is difficult to assess such liquidity changes when these

---

*All loans, all banks.

†M_{1B} plus savings deposits at commercial banks, small-denomination time deposits at commercial banks, and large-denomination time deposits at commercial banks (seasonally adjusted).

CHART 8-6 Banking liquidity and long-term interest rates.

series are expressed on an absolute basis, as in Chart 8-6. It has therefore been found more useful to express these data on a rate-of-change basis, as shown in Chart 8-7. A rate of change is calculated by dividing one month's data by another month in a previous period. In this case a 9-month rate of change has been used. Thus January 1981 would be divided by April 1980, March 1981 by July 1980, and so forth. The results are then plotted as an oscillator that fluctuates above and below a horizontal line at the 100 (unchanged) level.

The yield of Moody's Aaa bond yield has been plotted above this series for comparison. The close correlation between the two series is obvious, but there are enough discrepancies, such as the 1967–1968 period, when liquidity improved but debt markets deteriorated, to warn against following this particular indicator slavishly. Such a situation also underlines the point made earlier that a successful approach to forecasting interest rates can be accomplished only through an appraisal of the position of both the economic and financial indicators. In this particular period, as we will discover in a later chapter, the economic system remained in a position of tightness, thus outweighing the more positive aspect of the trend toward improving bank liquidity.

THE COMPOSITION OF BANK ASSETS AS A MEASURE OF LIQUIDITY

It was pointed out at the beginning of the chapter that liquidity really represents a ready source of cash. Since cash, in a balance-sheet sense, represents an asset, banking liquidity can also be measured by analyzing the quality of the asset side of the balance sheet of the banking system itself.

We know from a previous discussion that government securities and other investments of the best quality are the most liquid assets owned by banks while loans, which form the bulk of the assets, are the most illiquid and risky. Consequently, if we measure the relationship between loans and investments over a period of time, it is possible to discover whether the balance sheets of the banks are improving or deteriorating. If they are deteriorating, we would expect to see the proportion of loans, that is, poor-quality assets, rise against the total amount of assets held by banks and vice versa. This relationship (loans divided by total bank credit) is shown in Chart 8-8*a* on an absolute basis and in chart 8-8*b* on a 12-month rate-of-change basis. The series in Chart 8-8 has also been smoothed by a 6-month moving average to give it a less volatile trend and is plotted

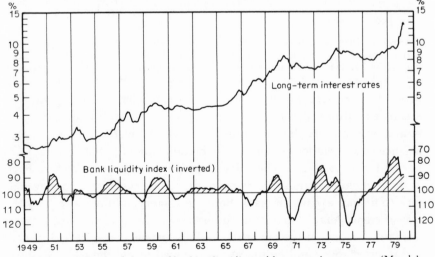

CHART 8-7   The rate of change of banking liquidity and long-term interest rates (Moody's Aaa corporates). *(Interest Rate Forecast.)*

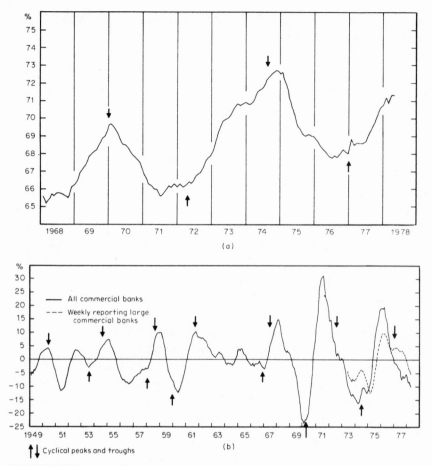

CHART 8-8   Bank liquidity. *(a)* Loans as a percentage of bank credit. Total bank credit is the sum of total loans and securities of all commercial loans. *(b)* Rate of change of bank liquidity. Bank credit less total loans, year-over-year change; adjusted for price inflation and smoothed. (Arrows indicate cyclical interest-rate peaks and troughs.) *(The Bank Credit Analyst.)*

inversely to correspond with interest-rate movements. A comparison of this index with the cyclical peaks and troughs of interest rates also represented on the chart shows that as the asset side of the banking-system balance sheet deteriorates and banks become more illiquid, interest rates have a tendency to rise. There are essentially two reasons for this. First, as the economy expands, the demand for loans picks up and corporations seek to finance expansion plans. Better business conditions also allay the fear of credit default, so that the proportion of loans to total bank assets increases. Second, at the top of the cycle banks begin to feel constrained, and in order to expand profits they are forced to sell the relatively low-yielding government securities using the newly released excess reserves to create more and higher-yielding loans, thereby accentuating the deterioration in their balance sheets.

As the recession unfolds, the quality of the banks' balance sheets improves. This is because the depressed business conditions associated with the recession encourage corporations and individuals to pay off their loans. Moreover, since recessionary periods are fraught with greater risk for holders of loan portfolios, the banks use their surplus funds to invest in good-quality government securities. Consequently the ratio between government securities and total bank credit improves dramatically in favor of the higher-quality government securities.

THE YIELD CURVE

One relatively simple method of measuring liquidity pressures is to study the relationship between the yield on short-term debt instruments and those at the long end. As discussed on page 27, the normal relationship is for yields to increase as the maturity of a debt instrument lengthens. This gives the yield curve its positive slope (see Figure 2-1).

Generally speaking, short-term interest rates are far more sensitive to business conditions and therefore subject to wider fluctuations than long-term yields. This can be seen from Chart 8-9, which shows the yields for 4- to 6-month commercial paper and Moody's Aaa long-term bonds. Peri-

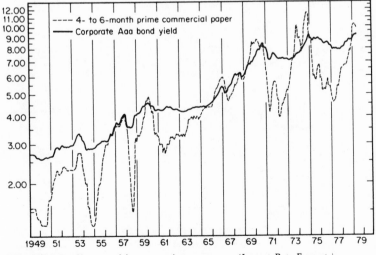

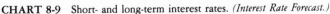

CHART 8-9 Short- and long-term interest rates. *(Interest Rate Forecast.)*

ods when short rates are falling sharply in relation to long rates are usually those when interest rates in general are falling and vice versa. Periods of financial squeeze develop when short rates move above long rates, as they did in 1959, 1966, 1969, 1973, and 1979. A quick cross-reference to other charts in this chapter will also show that such periods of a negative yield curve were also associated with deteriorating liquidity. With the exception of the period from late 1966 to early 1967, whenever short rates have fallen below those of the long end, this has signaled a return to easy money and lower interest rates. It has also represented a good point at which to purchase bonds.

On the other hand, when the difference between short- and long-term yields has begun to narrow on a cyclical basis, this has signaled that the economic and financial system has begun to tighten and that the major part of the bull market in bonds has ended. At such times the other economic and financial data should be closely monitored to determine a more precise time for the actual liquidation of bonds.

During the postwar period there has been a tendency not only for the period of this inverse yield curve to lengthen but also for the difference

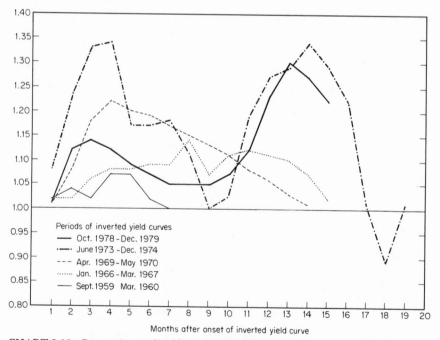

CHART 8-10   Postwar inverted yield curves. Ratio of 4- to 6-month prime commercial paper yield to Aaa corporate bond yield. *(Interest Rate Forecast.)*

between short and long rates to widen at successive cyclical interest-rate peaks. This relationship is illustrated in Chart 8-10.

SUMMARY

1. Liquidity can be thought of as cash reserves or the ability of a corporation, individual, or government to meet demand for payment.

2. The level of interest rates is affected by the absolute level of liquidity in the financial system.

3. The movement of interest rates is determined by the rate of change of liquidity, that is, the speed at which the money supply-demand relationship changes.

4. Liquidity can be measured in a number of ways, but the most useful and timely data are derived from the banking system. The two most useful series to monitor from the point of view of forecasting interest rate changes are the deposit-loan ratio and changes in the level of government securities held by banks.

9
INTEREST RATES
AND THE ECONOMY

In forecasting interest rates one of the most important areas to concentrate on is the level and direction of economic activity. A trend toward growing slackness in the economy results in lower interest rates, while economic growth that results in tightness and capacity shortages puts upward pressure on rates. The task of understanding and forecasting economic trends may seem overpowering to the average investor at first, especially as professional economists armed with batteries of econometric models have a reputation for being poor forecasters. Fortunately economics can be a relatively simple matter of common sense, and a number of institutions, both public and private, publish many of the key economic indicators (in easy-to-read chart form), which have proved useful for forecasting interest-rate trends. When reporting economic statistics the media tend to emphasize significant changes on a month-by-month basis, but from the point of view of forecasting interest rates it is the *trend* of an economic indicator over a number of months that is important rather than an isolated monthly figure. This is because economies take a number of months to reverse direction and because the data reported for any particular month may well be distorted by some temporary phenomenon. Before considering the interplay of these various indicators with the trend of interest rates, it is important to understand something about the relationship between interest rates and the economy.

INTEREST RATES AND THE LEVEL
OF ECONOMIC ACTIVITY

Figure 9-1 shows an idealized business cycle. The horizontal line represents a period of equilibrium, or no growth, in the economy. The sine wave moving above and below this line indicates periods of growth and contraction in business activity. When the wave is above the horizontal line and rising, it indicates not only that business activity is rising but that it is expanding faster and faster. When the line is falling but is still above the equilibrium level, it represents an expanding economy but one that is expanding more and more slowly, until eventually the rate of growth falls below the line, pointing up a period of economic contraction.

As long as the wave is below the horizontal line, it indicates negative growth in business activity. A rising line indicates that the rate of contraction is declining until the wave reaches and eventually rises above the horizontal line, at which time the economy begins to expand.

Figure 9-2 shows the relationship of the interest-rate cycle to the business cycle. As the economy begins to expand (i.e., crosses above the equilibrium line), the surplus economic capacity which developed out of the previous recession begins to get used up, so that in the relatively early stage of the economic cycle the demand for credit and supply of credit come into balance and upward pressure is placed on its price, namely, interest rates. This juncture is illustrated in Figure 9-2 by the downward-pointing arrow; it indicates the low point in the cycle for interest rates, which of course represents the high point for bonds. In practice, since short-term interest rates are very sensitive to business conditions, they have a tendency to trough out some time ahead of the long end of the debt market. In the

FIGURE 9-1 An idealized business cycle.

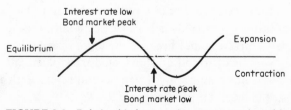

FIGURE 9-2 Relationship between interest-rate cycle and business cycle.

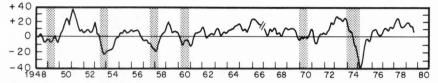

CHART 9-1   Net changes in inventories on hand in 1972 dollars, smoothed; annual rate in billions of dollars. This series is a weighted four-term moving average with weights 1, 2, 2, 1 placed on the terminal month of the span. This chart shows how erratic the movement of inventories can be. The shaded areas represent periods of economic recession. *(Business Conditions Digest.)*

1972–1974 bear market, for example, 4- to 6-month commercial paper yields reached their low in April 1972 while long-term AAA bonds did not really begin their bear phase until the end of that year.

As the economy continues to expand, tightness in the economic system becomes more severe, and so the price of money continues to rise. The rise is not usually a one-way affair since the process of economic expansion is not one of uninterrupted advance. This is because the economy adjusts to new levels of activity along the way. Quite often, for example, businesspeople will experience sharply higher sales and respond to this development by ordering additional inventories, often far in excess of what the expanded sales rate justifies. This temporary increase in the demand on resources has the effect of fueling loan demand and putting upward pressure on interest rates. However, since the corporations eventually realize that the rate of growth in sales cannot be sustained, they cut their inventories to more sensible levels and begin to pay off some of the loans that were used to finance them, that is, reduce their demand for credit, which has the effect of lowering interest rates. This is one example of how the overall expansion rate in the economy may be temporarily interrupted, creating countercyclical declines in interest rates. Inventory adjustments are probably the most common cause of temporary aberrations (see Chart 9-1). Others might be abrupt changes in the pattern of government expenditure, oil shortages, accelerated consumer buying in anticipation of a tax change, extreme winter weather conditions, and the like.

Figure 9-2 shows that interest rates still have a tendency to rise even after the economy has reached its maximum rate of expansion. It is not until the economy has entered the recessionary stage that enough slack has developed in the system to permit lower interest rates. Figure 9-3 shows that the declining phase of the economy is also characterized by a process of irregular decline and correction, just as the expanding part was.

If these temporary adjustments did not occur, forecasting interest rates would be a relatively simple affair, but given the confusing crosscurrents that develop from time to time, it is often difficult to judge whether a

FIGURE 9-3   Declining phase of the economy.

turning point is one of cyclical or intermediate, that is, temporary, proportion. Because of the rapid economic adjustment that usually results from these short-run factors, changes in the level of interest rates will often develop quickly. Because most economic data are reported with at least a 6-week to 2-month lag, the countercyclical movement in interest rates has often occurred well before any action can be taken. For this reason our approach here will concentrate on the primary or cyclical trend in interest rates, since these turning points take considerably longer to develop. In addition, the indicators that will be considered have historically had a long lead time over interest-rate peaks and troughs, so that it is often possible to establish that their trend has reversed, thereby developing greater confidence that the cyclical trend of interest rates has also changed.

USING THE INDICATORS TO FORECAST INTEREST RATES

As discussed in earlier chapters, since there is no single area that can be used alone to forecast interest rates accurately, the economic-indicator approach can succeed only if a number of indicators are considered together to establish a consensus picture of the economy as it applies to interest-rate movements. The reliance on one particular indicator, however useful it may have been in the past, does not guarantee success for the future. This is because each business cycle has a characteristic or structure unique to itself, so that the weight of a particular sector of the economy may be different from one cycle to the next, as a result of institutional changes, distortions resulting from inflation, and so forth. For example, in the business cycle that began in 1970, the importance of the housing industry was far greater than in the 1966–1970 cycle. National defense purchases as a percentage of the GNP rose from 7 to 9 percent between 1965 and 1968, yet by 1979 they had fallen to less than 5 percent. The changed importance of these two indicators is shown in Chart 9-2.

Naturally with a myriad of statistics and indicators to consider, it is necessary to try to pick out the most important. We shall therefore concentrate on the following:

- Manufacturing Capacity Utilization, a general measure of economic slackness

- Composite Index of Lagging Indicators, a measure of overall strength or weakness in the economy

- Help Wanted Advertising, a measure of the demand for labor

- Housing Starts and Commercial and Construction Contracts, two indicators that are sensitive to credit demands

- Manufacturing Sales-Inventory Ratio, which monitors financial pressure in the corporate sector because of excessive inventories

- The Composite Index of Leading Indicators, which gives long leads between interest-rate peaks and troughs

Easy access to each of these indicators can be obtained through a subscription (about $40) to the *Business Conditions Digest* (BCD), published monthly by the Commerce Department. The BCD contains a wealth of information on all aspects of the economy in statistical form, and back data for most indicators are available for the whole postwar period. The real value of the BCD, however, is the many excellent charts of virtually all the important indicators. Recessionary areas are shaded, so that it is possible to gain some kind of perspective on how the various indicators lead or lag the overall economy. Chart 9-3, for example, illustrates some of the main

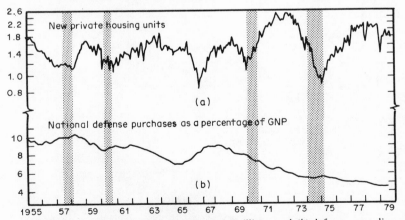

CHART 9-2   *(a)* Housing starts, annual rate, in millions, and *(b)* defense expenditure as a percentage of the GNP, Q. This chart shows how the level of housing starts varies from recovery to recovery. The influence of defense expenditure on economic conditions has altered radically from 1955 to 1979, as shown in the chart. The shaded areas represent periods of recessions. *(Business Conditions Digest.)*

bond-yield series and shows how the various cyclical interest peaks have occurred either at the onset of a recession or during the middle of one.

SOME SIMPLE STATISTICAL TECHNIQUES

Before considering these indicators individually, it is worth discussing a few simple statistical techniques that help cast the data in a more useful form. It is not the intention here to introduce complicated mathematical formulas since they are unnecessary and would complicate matters unduly, but since the business of forecasting interest rates correctly can be very

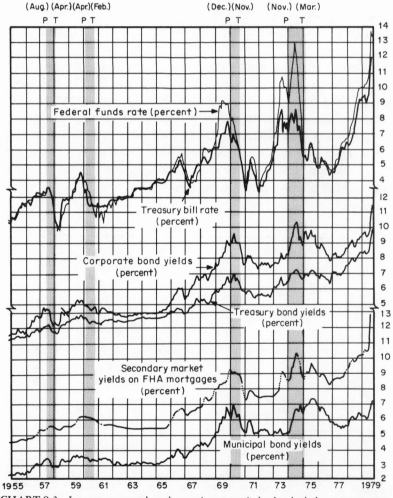

CHART 9-3   Interest-rate trends and recessionary periods; the shaded areas represent recessions. *(Business Conditions Digest.)*

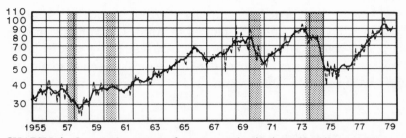

CHART 9-4   Construction contracts for commercial and industrial buildings in millions of square feet of floor area, MCD moving five-term average. *(Business Conditions Digest.)*

profitable, it is well worth taking a few moments to consider some techniques that will make the task much easier.

MOVING AVERAGES

Reference to Chart 9-4 shows the monthly values of construction contract awards, represented by the dashed line. Since the series is extremely volatile, it is difficult to identify cyclical turning points until well after the fact. One helpful technique is to calculate a moving average. An average is calculated by totaling a number of months of data and dividing that total by the number of months concerned. For example, if the observations for January to May are 10, 11, 12, 13, and 14, the total will be 60 and the average 12.0 (60 ÷ 5). The average is made to "move" by adding the June observation, dropping January's, and dividing this new total by 5 (the number of observations is always the divisor). This then becomes a five-period (in this case 5-month) moving average. The difference this smoothing makes is illustrated by the solid line in Chart 9-4 showing the construction and contracts series. Not all the fluctuations have been eliminated, but the data have been smoothed enough to move easily, identifying major turning points.

A data series can be smoothed by any number of periods, and the longer the period the more efficient the smoothing. There is a trade-off, however, since the longer the period the less sensitive the data will be and the more delayed the turning points. The trick is to calculate a moving average that balances the advantages of smoothing with the disadvantages of the loss of sensitivity. Of course, this will depend upon the characteristics of the various series, but generally a 3-, 4-, 6-, or 9-month smoothing will prove to be the most efficient for our purpose.

Strictly speaking, the average for any particular period really relates to the halfway mark of that period. For example a 7-month moving average for the January–July period actually lies in April, or halfway between January and July, and should be plotted in April. The 5-month moving average shown on Chart 9-4 has in fact been centered or plotted at the halfway mark, but for our purpose here it is more convenient to plot the moving average for the latest month used in the calculation, that is, July.

DEVIATION FROM TREND

Chart 9-5 shows the Composite Index of Lagging Indicators from 1948 to 1980. Because of the tremendous economic growth in the postwar period this index shows a more or less uninterrupted trend of growth and fails to emphasize cyclical swings fully. Consequently in its raw state it does not appear to be particularly useful for forecasting interest rates. Ideally it would be more helpful if this indicator could be reconstructed so that it would oscillate above and below a central reference point like the hypothetical sine wave in Figure 9-1. This can easily be achieved by relating the monthly data to a moving average. This technique is known as a *deviation from trend,* the trend being the moving average and the deviation being the the movement above or below the moving average. The deviation is calculated by dividing the monthly observation by the moving average. Figure 9-4 shows a series combined with a moving average in the top portion and the same series expressed as a percentage of that moving average at the bottom. When the actual series crosses above and below the moving average, the deviation-from-trend series moves above and below its 100

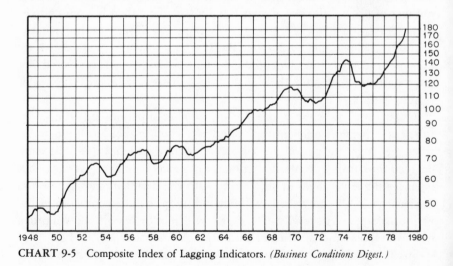

CHART 9-5 Composite Index of Lagging Indicators. *(Business Conditions Digest.)*

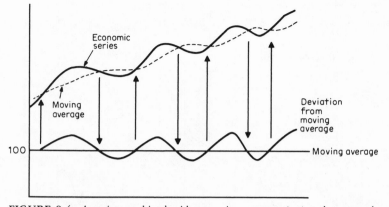

FIGURE 9-4 A series combined with a moving average *(top)* and expressed as a percentage of that moving average *(bottom)*.

reference line. The vertical arrows on the chart indicate these crossover points.

The moving average calculated for a deviation series can be for any period, but empirically 12-, 24-, and 48-month periods have proved the most useful. The 48-month period is particularly helpful since it is approximately the length of the average business cycle.

Besides accentuating the cyclicality of a series, the deviation-from-trend approach often has the advantage of signaling a cyclical change in direction several months ahead of the actual series. By comparing current readings with historical ones it is also possible to determine the degree of tightness or slackness in that particular sector compared with previous cycles.

THE INDICATORS

MANUFACTURING CAPACITY UTILIZATION

The Federal Reserve publishes several measures of capacity utilization, but the most useful for forecasting interest rates is that of Manufacturing Capacity Utilization since it is a relatively broad measure of economic slackness. A 30-year history of this indicator with Moody's Aaa bond yields is shown in Chart 9-6. A horizontal line at 82.5 percent has also been drawn on the chart as a rough indication of the level at which high utilization rates put upward pressure on interest rates. This is a very simple but effective measure, for when the utilization rate is at an extreme reading of

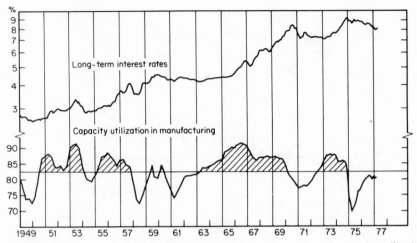

CHART 9-6   Long-term interest rates (Moody's Aaa corporates) versus capacity utilization rates; data from Federal Reserve Board. *(Interest Rate Forecast.)*

75 percent, one can be fairly confident that interest rates are likely to continue their decline for some time since it would take several months to push the capacity measure over the 82.5 percent reading. Similarly readings of 90 percent or more, which indicate tight levels of capacity, point up the high probability that rates will continue to rise for at least several months in view of the relatively long time required to generate the degree of economic slackness traditionally associated with an interest peak. One note of caution: over the years the basis on which this series has been calculated has changed. For example, as a result of the OPEC oil crisis in 1973–1974 a significant amount of plant capacity became obsolescent but was still counted in the capacity utilization figures published by the Federal Reserve. Consequently many economists felt that the low levels of capacity utilization indicated by the *published* figures were actually *understating* the real levels, thereby offering amore bearish outlook for the bond market than might be warranted by the facts.

COMPOSITE INDEX OF LEADING INDICATORS

Over the years economists have classified many economic indicators according to their chronological position in the business cycle. Some, for example, are more sensitive to changes in activity than others. They lead business activity and are consequently known as *leading indicators.* Those that rise and fall at approximately the same time as the economy are called *coincident indicators,* while those whose response is somewhat delayed are classified as *lagging indicators.* Housing starts, corporate profits, and help wanted advertising are examples of leading indicators; industrial production, personal income, and manufacturing sales are coincident indicators; and capital spending and unemployment are examples of lagging indicators.

To help the analytical process the Department of Commerce has grouped together a number of indicators according to these three classifications. As discussed earlier, interest rates are a lagging indicator since they reach their peak well after the economy has turned down and experience their low point after the expansion has been under way for some time. For this reason it is useful initially to consider an indicator with a relatively long lead time over interest-rate peaks and troughs. The Composite Index of Leading Indicators (Chart 9-7) is therefore quite useful in this respect. The arrows above and below this series show the cyclical peaks and troughs of the leading indicators. At first sight the relationship is not especially meaningful since the lead times are extremely long, particularly at interest-rate peaks. On the other hand, if the indicators are plotted as a deviation from a moving average, some more helpful conclusions can be drawn for timing interest-rate peaks. Chart 9-8 demonstrates this point quite clearly. We have already seen that in order for a meaningful peak in interest rates to develop it is necessary for considerable slack to develop in the economic system first. Taken in its raw state, the Index of Leading Indicators does not give much help in this direction since it normally turns down well ahead of such a development. On the other hand, when this

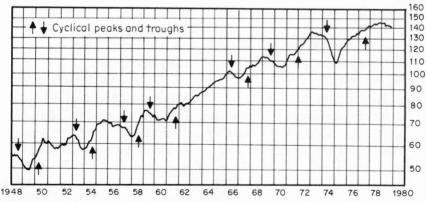

CHART 9-7   Composite Index of Leading Indicators versus interest-rate peaks and troughs. *(Business Conditions Digest.)*

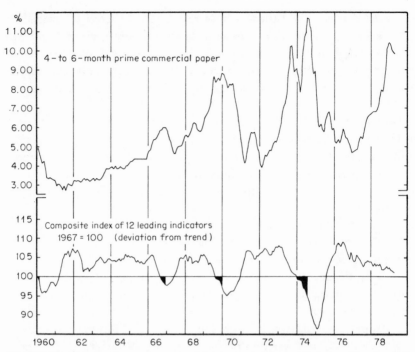

CHART 9-8 Four- to six-month commercial paper versus Composite Index of Leading Indicators. *(Interest Rate Forecast.)*

indicator is plotted as a deviation from a 12-month moving average, it introduces some cyclicality into the index: in other words, the index behaves like the idealized business cycle shown in Figure 9-1.

In this case the moving average, shown here as the horizontal line at 100, represents a rough sort of equlibrium level. When the index is above the 100 line, it means that it is *above* its 12-month moving average, and when it is below the line, it is *below* its 12-month moving average.

The important point for forecasting is that since the 1950s the cyclical peak in interest rates has always occurred *only after the leading indicators* have fallen below their horizontal reference line (the 12-month moving average). The lead time between this crossover and the actual peak in interest rates is represented by the shaded area. This lead time has varied from as little as 2 months in 1960 to as much as 7 months in 1974.

While this approach, like virtually all the others discussed here, does not give a precise timing of interest-rate turning points, it does at least tell us within a few months when a peak might be expected. Until the deviated series falls below the 100 reference line marking its 12-month moving average, empirical evidence suggests that it is highly unlikely that the economy has contracted sufficiently to be consistent with a curtailment of credit demands and therefore a peak in the interest-rate cycle.

A regular feature of the *Interest Rate Forecast* is shown in Chart 9-9, illustrating four important series that have proved useful for forecasting

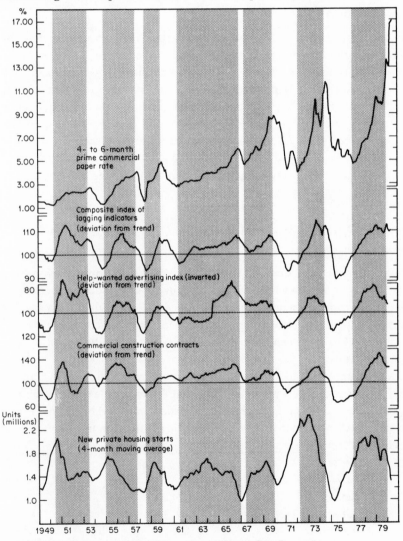

CHART 9-9 Interest rates and the economy. *(Interest Rate Forecast.)*

trends in interest rates with a monthly average of the yield on 4- to 6-month commercial paper. Certain portions of the chart have been shaded to represent periods of rising interest rates, helping to point up the leading characteristics of these indicators.

HOUSING STARTS

Housing starts, shown at the bottom of Chart 9-9, have been smoothed by a 4-month moving average. This indicator has the longest lead time of the four shown on the chart. The lead time at peaks has ranged between 9 and 32 months, averaging 16 months. Housing is a very important sector of the economy not only since new housing developments are a prime demander of mortgage money but also because purchase of a new house is also responsible for second-round effects on the economy such as increased demand for consumer durables, furniture, and the like. New housing starts have also had a relatively long lead time at interest-rate troughs.

COMMERCIAL AND CONSTRUCTION CONTRACTS

This useful credit-sensitive indicator monitors nonresidential construction. Its average lead time for interest-rate peaks of 6 months has been somewhat shorter than that of new housing starts, probably because it reflects the capital spending habits of corporations, which is a lagging indicator. The lead time of commercial and construction contracts at interest-rate troughs has been very short and has occasionally lagged by 1 or 2 months.

This indicator is shown here as a deviation from a moving average. It is worth noting at interest-rate troughs that the lead time of this indicator has tended to be far greater when it has fallen considerably below trend, that is, the 100 reference line, since this type of situation usually indicates an economic recession in which a substantial amount of economic slack has built up.

HELP WANTED ADVERTISING

The Index of Help Wanted Advertising is published by the Conference Board, a nonprofit economic foundation sponsored by major corporations.

It measures the amount of classified job advertising devoted to job offers throughout the country. It is considered a leading economic indicator and is an excellent pointer to the trend of the demand for labor and also of general business conditions. Its performance can be traced back to the 1920s, and this index has led the peak in interest rates in every business cycle since that time. Help wanted advertising is represented on Chart 9-9 as a deviation from a 48-month moving average. In the post-1949 period shown on the chart, the lead time of this indicator against interest-rate peaks has ranged from 6 to 22 months, with an average lead time of 12 months. As with the other indicators, lead times at interest-rate troughs are somewhat smaller, averaging 7½ months during this 30-year period.

COMPOSITE INDEX OF LAGGING INDICATORS

This composite index is also plotted as a deviation from a moving average. It monitors general strength or weakness in the economy and has had an average lead time of 10 months at interest-rate peaks, which has ranged from 2 to 28 months. Its lead time has been considerably shorter at interest-rate troughs and has even lagged on some occasions, but it is worth noting that except for the 1958–1959 interest-rate rise, advances in interest rates have been very limited while this index has remained below its trend. In this context the lagging indicators have proved to be very useful in confirming that a cyclical rise in interest rates is under way, for while many of the other indexes have had relatively long lead times at interest-rate troughs, it is unusual for a trough to have developed while the lagging index has remained below its trend. In this respect the 1975–1977 period should be considered. At the end of 1975 most of the indicators represented on Chart 9-9 had been rising for a period far longer than their average postwar lead time. At this point it would have been easy to buy the argument that interest rates had troughed, but as it turned out they still had another year in which to fall. However, the lagging index at this time was still well below its trend (100 reference line). It was not until the end of 1976 that it crossed above its trend, thereby indicating a more general tightening in the system sufficient to put upward pressure on interest rates.

This example points up the need to use economic indicators as a group for the purpose of forming an opinion, since the lead times between their individual peaks and troughs and those of cyclical turning points for interest rates can vary considerably.

THE SALES-INVENTORY RATIO

The sales-inventory ratio (Chart 9-10) is useful for forecasting interest-rate peaks only. This indicator measures the ratio of manufacturers' sales to their inventories. Generally speaking, as long as this ratio is declining, it represents a healthy financial picture for corporations since it points up that sales are rising faster than inventories. A rising ratio implies that inventories are at an uncomfortable level since they are being covered by lower and lower sales.

A rising sales-inventory ratio can really be classified into two phases. At first the ratio advances because inventories are rising at a faster pace than sales. This implies that corporations are starting to come under financial pressure since the revenues from the sales are not expanding fast enough to cover the outlay on additional inventories. This growing deficit is usually financed through the banking system in the form of loans, thereby putting upward pressure on interest rates. As business conditions deteriorate, sales begin to slow considerably but corporations still have to take delivery of inventories ordered some months before. At this point the squeeze intensifies since the corporation can control neither the falling sales nor the rising level of previously ordered inventories. This process is known as *involuntary inventory accumulation* since the corporation does not want the inventory but is still committed to accepting it. In terms of the

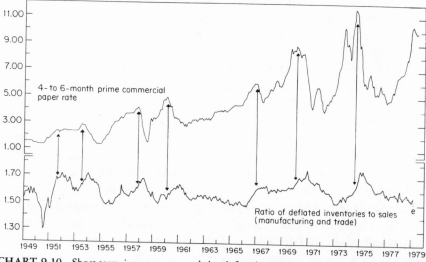

CHART 9-10   Short-term interest rates and the deflated-inventory–sales ratio. *(Interest Rate Forecast.)*

interest-rate cycle this point often marks the interest-rate peak and in some cases actually accentuates it, for although economic activity has subsided sufficiently to bring normal credit demands into balance, the forced demand for money arising from the involuntary-inventory-accumulation phase adds an air of panic as corporations scramble to obtain funds at virtually any price.

The second phase of an advancing sales-inventory ratio is less important for forecasting interest rates because it develops when sales are still declining in relation to inventories, but since both are falling (sales faster than inventories), total credit demands for inventories are now decreasing, which results in downward pressure on interest rates.

The main conclusion to be drawn from this discussion of the sales-inventory ratio is that a rising ratio is almost always a prerequisite for a peak in interest rates, as shown in Chart 9-10. The difficulty, however, is distinguishing between the first phase and the situation when inventories are actually declining.

One clue is sometimes given by the relationship between commercial and industrial bank loans and all other bank loans. Chart 9-11 shows the rate of change of the various measures of loan growth with the monthly average of the yield on 4- to 6-month commercial paper. The second loan series shows the rate of growth of commercial and industrial loans. Corporations borrow money from banks on a short-term basis for a variety of reasons, but the predominant influence on the direction and level of this series is changes in inventories. The loan series next to the bottom one is for all loans other than those which fall in the commercial and industrial category and is therefore a good proxy for general credit demands. Reference to Chart 9-11 shows that most of the time both series rise and fall together. If the economy was experiencing an involuntary inventory accumulation, commercial and industrial loans would be expected to expand, with other loans either falling or remaining steady (in terms of growth rate). Chart 9-11 shows that these characteristics did materialize just before the 1966 and 1974 interest-rate peaks, at which time the commercial and industrial loan series actually made a secondary peak. With the 1969 interest-rate top the commercial and industrial loan series did not form a secondary peak, but its cyclical high lagged the other series by several months. While a divergence between these two loan series is not a prerequisite for an interest-rate peak, its development, when confirmed by a sharp rise in the sales-inventory ratio, is a strong indication that the end of the bear market in debt securities is at hand.

It should be remembered that these indicators represent loan *growth*

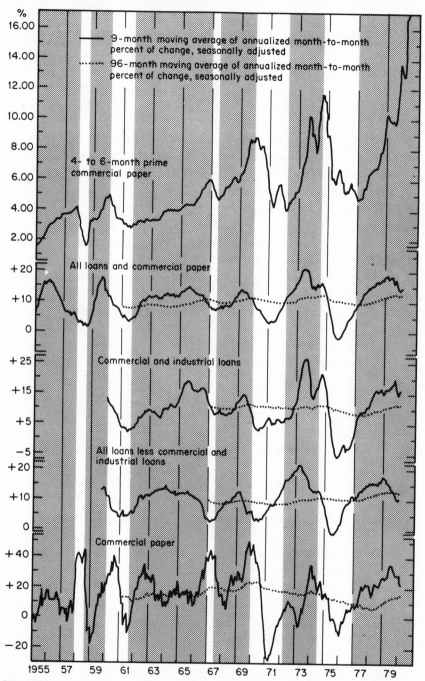

CHART 9-11 Short-term interest rates and four measures of loan growth for all commercial banks. *(Interest Rate Forecast.)*

rather than the actual amount of loans outstanding, which explains why they lead interest-rate peaks and troughs rather than coinciding with them or lagging behind.

SUMMARY

1. Interest-rate trends are closely tied to developments in the business cycle. When surplus slack has been used up, an expanding economy results in a trend toward higher interest rates and vice versa.

2. It can be empirically shown that certain economic indicators which monitor general levels of economic activity, tightness, or slackness in the system or are particularly credit-sensitive can be used as leading indicators for the cyclical turning points of interest rates.

3. The usefulness of many of these indicators can be improved through staistical techniques which smooth the data or accentuate the cyclical movements of these series.

4. The indicators should not be used in isolation however reliable their forecasting record has been in the past. They should be incorporated into the analysis as a group and combined with the techniques discussed in other chapters.

10
INTEREST RATES AND PRICE INFLATION

Interest rates and the rate of price inflation usually move in the same direction. This is because an interest rate is the price paid for renting money, and if the money itself is depreciating in terms of its purchasing power, the lender requires more rent as compensation for this loss.

For example, investors who have money available to lend are likely to incorporate an inflation premium into the interest rate they are prepared to accept. If the expected rate of price inflation is 8 percent, both sides of the transaction recognize that in 12 months their money will be worth only about 92 percent of its current value. The lender naturally wishes to be compensated for this loss in value in the form of a higher interest rate, while the borrower will be prepared to pay a higher rate as a result of the potential currency depreciation.

This inflation factor gains importance the longer the maturity of the debt security concerned. For example, since the rate of price inflation is relatively stable over a few months, there is little inflation risk with a 90-day T-bill or other short-term debt instrument compared with a 20- or 30-year bond, where the uncertainty becomes considerably greater. In the early 1960s, for example, inflation rates were hardly noticeable, but by the late 1970s price inflation rates had risen to well over 8 percent. If the current interest rate does not include a sufficient premium to cover the expected inflation rate, prospective lenders will turn to other financial instruments such as equities, real estate, or gold. Therefore, at some point enough funds are diverted from the bond and money markets to lead to a shortage of lendable funds, causing interest rates to rise sufficiently to cover the inflation premium.

This normally occurs at the end of the interest-rate cycle, when money is getting progressively tighter. Later, when economic activity is dipping sufficiently to cause downward pressure on many of the alternative financial assets, bonds and other debt instruments become a progressively more attractive alternative. The decline in economic activity therefore results in lower inflation and inflationary expectations and encourages money to flow back to the debt markets from competitive investment sources. Because of this sharp change in the supply-demand relationship for money, interest-rate peaks are usually very pointed as rates rise up to their final cyclical summit and then fall just as sharply.

At interest-rate troughs this process is usually a much quieter and rounder affair, since economic and inflationary pressures take a long time to build up momentum.

The relationship between interest rates and price inflation can be observed in a longer-term sense by comparing Charts 5-3 and 5-4. Chart 5-4 shows the very long-term cycles in interest rates over the last 200 years, and Chart 5-3 shows wholesale prices over a similar period. Interest rates made a secular peak in the 1860s along with wholesale prices. Both series fell in the 1880s, rose in the early part of the twentieth century, and fell again in the 1930s. The postwar period has experienced an upward cycle of both interest rates and prices which, as of late 1980, had shown few signs of abating.

While it can clearly be shown that there is a long-term relationship between interest rates and price inflation, it is difficult to come up with any statistical techniques useful for relating the rate of change of prices with the trend of interest rates for the purpose of forecasting cyclical peaks and troughs of the debt markets. There are three reasons for this: (1) Price changes become very volatile toward the end of the business cycle so that it is very easy to become whipsawed. (2) The lag between the peak in the rate of change of prices and the cyclical peak in interest rates is often insufficient to offer reliable and consistent signals. (3) Perhaps the most important of all in a shorter term sense, that is, over a period of 3 to 4 months or so, the relationship between prices and interest rates is very imprecise because of the differing forces that affect these two items over brief periods. Moreover, it is the *expected* rate of inflation that affects interest rates over the short term rather than the reported figures.

This somewhat imprecise relationship can be seen from Chart 10-1, which shows 4- to 6-month commercial paper with a 12-month rate of change of the Consumer Price Index. In 1969 and 1976 the Consumer Price Index led the interest-rate peak, but in the 1966 cycle it coincided with it.

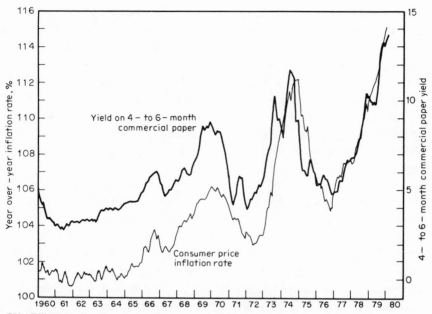

CHART 10-1 Four- to six-month paper versus the Consumer Price Index, 12-month rate of change.

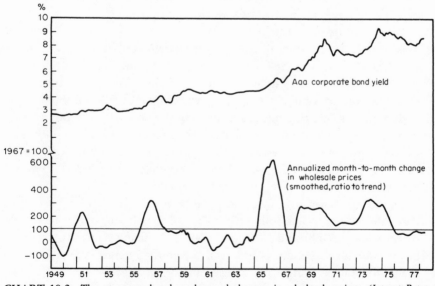

CHART 10-2 The corporate bond market and changes in wholesale prices. *(Interest Rate Forecast.)*

The essential problem with using this measurement of price inflation can be seen from closer reference to the 1974 experience. During the summer of 1974 the interest rate series began to fall sharply, but it was not until the decline was well underway that the inflation rate peaked.

An alternative to using the Consumer Price Index is to take wholesale prices, since they are more of a leading indicator of price inflation. Since this series is extremely volatile, it must be smoothed to filter out many misleading signals. In Chart 10-2 the monthly percentage changes in the Wholesale Price Index have been smoothed twice, first by a 12-month moving average and then by a 6-month average. This smoothing in turn has been divided by a 96-month moving average, like the loan series described in Chapter 6. This is a fairly complex and tedious way of treating price inflation figures, but the chart nevertheless shows that each of the cyclical interest-rate peaks under review was preceded by a peak in the wholesale price series. The problem is that the lead times can vary from as little as a few months, as in 1974, to well over 1 year, as in 1953. It should be pointed out that since this is a deviation-from-trend measurement, the important thing to look for is the direction of the movement. To compare the actual levels of this indicator between one cycle and another will prove misleading. Consequently the very high reading in 1965–1966 does not mean that the inflation rate was at its highest in that period, for quite clearly much higher rises were seen in later cycles.

One more useful measurement from the point of view of forecasting interest-rate peaks can be obtained from statistics published in the *Business Conditions Digest* on sensitive wholesale prices. This measurement, shown in Chart 10-3, is a diffusion index. A diffusion index measures the percentage of a given number of items that are above or below their levels over a given period. In this case the index is measuring the percentage of the twenty-two items with sensitive prices that are above their levels of 9 months ago. Consequently if all the items are higher in price than they were 9 months before, the diffusion index would have a reading of 100. If each item was below or at the same level, the reading would be 0.

From the interest-rate-forecasting point of view it is important to note that interest-rate peaks follow the point of maximum inflationary pressures as measured by the diffusion index. Thus many items started to fall below their levels 9 months ago, well before the interest-rate peak began to fall, thereby pointing up that the economy has already begun to weaken sufficiently to put downward pressure on prices and therefore interest rates. Although this approach cannot be used as a precise timing device for

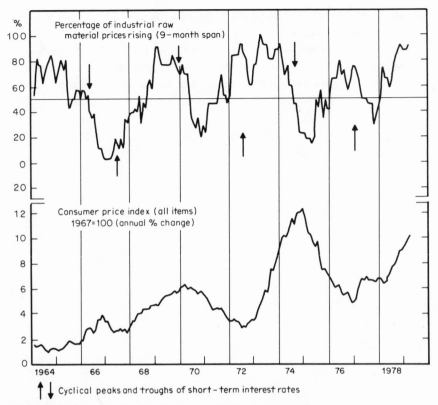

CHART 10-3   Two indicators of inflation. *(The Bank Credit Analyst.)*

identifying an interest-rate peak since the leading characteristics of the index vary considerably from cycle to cycle, nevertheless it symbolizes the need for inflationary pressures to abate before it is safe to assume that an interest peak is at hand. In this respect, a drop in this index below the 50 percent level has often proved to be an important condition for a cyclical peak in interest rates.

CONCLUSION

It is important to understand that there is a basic connection between the trend of price inflation and the trend of interest rates. Since this relationship is difficult to measure over relatively short periods of time, the incorporation of a measure of price inflation into the overall analysis is useful therefore only as background information.

Readers are better advised to concentrate on liquidity trends and changes in the level of economic activity, both of which are useful gauges of inflationary pressures in the system and far easier to monitor.

11
EXTERNAL INFLUENCES ON INTEREST-RATE TRENDS

So far the factors affecting interest rates have all been domestically oriented, but it is important to understand that developments outside the United States can influence both the trend and level of American interest rates. This is because the economies of the world are closely interwoven and there is an almost free flow of capital from one country to another. In recent years the floating-currency system has also placed more immediate pressure on governments to respond to external developments.

While previous chapters have tried to offer some practical guidance, the material covered in this chapter will be more useful as background information since meaningful data on a country's external position is reported only well after the fact. It is very difficult, if not impossible, to use the data to determine the trend of domestic interest rates precisely because external forces must, by definition, involve a relationship with other countries, which also should be analyzed, and because in a vast majority of cases external developments exacerbate rather than originate a cyclical trend in the level of interest rates.

THE GLOBAL ECONOMY

There has always been a world trade cycle in the sense that most countries go through approximately the same stage of the business cycle together and are therefore subject to many of the same pressures. Charts 11-1 and 11-2 illustrate the close connection between the commodity prices and interest rates of several countries in the nineteenth century. In recent years

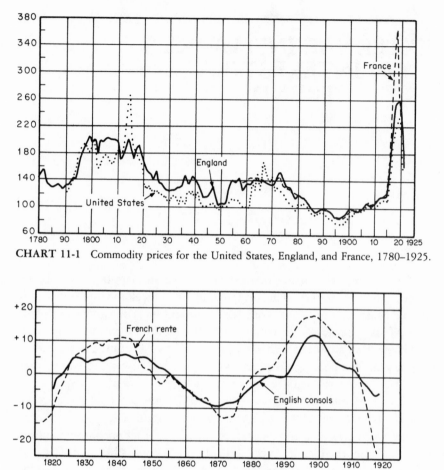

CHART 11-1   Commodity prices for the United States, England, and France, 1780–1925.

CHART 11-2   Interest rates for the United Kingdom and France, 1815–1925.

the relationship between these individual cycles and the global business cycle have become even closer with the advent of freer capital markets, free floating currencies, better communications, joint government policy moves, and the like. The characteristics and timing of each country's economic recovery naturally differ somewhat from the world cycle due to different economic structures, individual monetary policies, and so forth. However, their progress is relatively similar, as can be seen from Chart 11-3, which shows the trend of industrial production for some of the major countries since 1956.

Given that the majority of the industrialized economies are usually moving in the same direction, it follows that there is also a global interest-rate cycle as well.

Charts 11-4 to 11-6 show long- and short-term interest rates for several countries. While specific developments have caused the interest rate of individual countries to move away from the general pattern temporarily, there is still a common bond between them all. Having established the general relationship between the interest rates and the economies of the various countries, we will find it appropriate to examine the mechanism of their interrelationships.

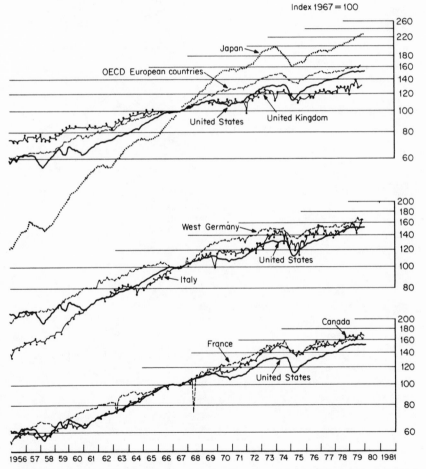

CHART 11-3   Trends of industrial production for selected industrialized countries. *(Business Conditions Digest.)*

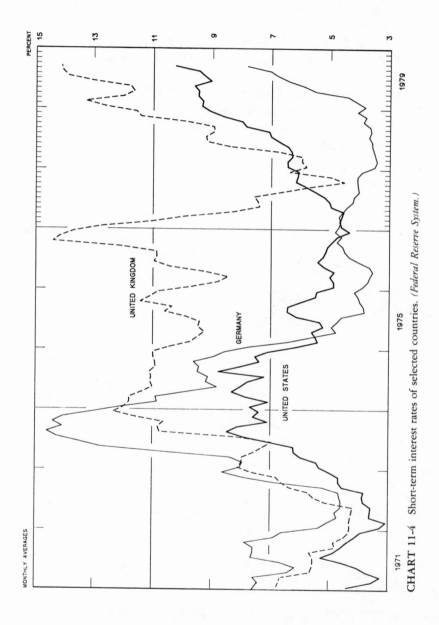

CHART 11-4 Short-term interest rates of selected countries. *(Federal Reserve System.)*

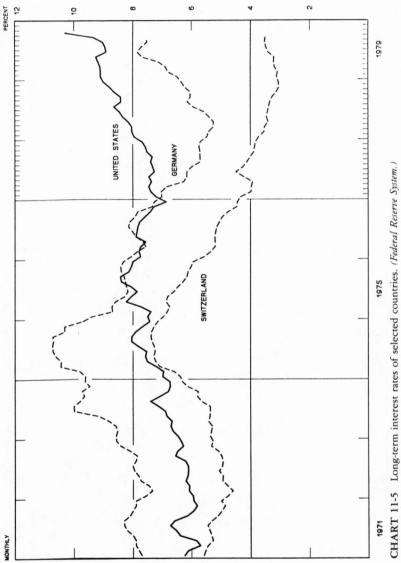

CHART 11-5 Long-term interest rates of selected countries. *(Federal Reserve System.)*

135

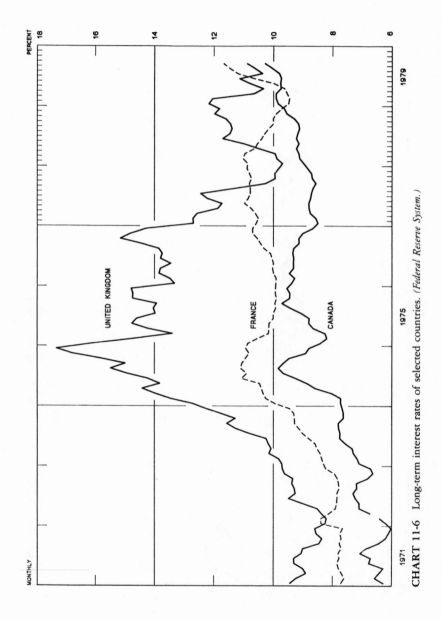

CHART 11-6 Long-term interest rates of selected countries. *(Federal Reserve System.)*

136

INTEREST RATES AND CURRENCY MOVEMENTS

The external value of a country's currency is determined by the supply-and-demand relationship for that currency. This relationship is established through the balance of payments, which is the sum total of a country's financial transactions with the rest of the world. It can be divided into the current account and the capital account.

THE CURRENT ACCOUNT

The current account consists of all trade in goods and services including interest and dividend payments, tourist spending or receipts, and the like. Often a country with a strengthening economy relative to the rest of the world will have a current account that is weakening, in that the surplus is getting smaller or the deficit is getting larger. This is because a strong economy has a propensity to increase imports while the exporting sectors of the economy have less of an incentive to export and prefer to concentrate on the more profitable home market. Other things being equal, the current account will deteriorate as an economy gains momentum *relative to its trading partners,* and this will put downward pressure on its currency. It is important to stress the fact that the economic momentum should be strong in a relative sense rather than in an absolute one since the movement of the current account is caused by the competition of one country with a group of others for a basket of goods and services.

Change in the value of a country's currency can have a profound change on the level of interest rates for several reasons. First, if a currency depreciates, it means that upward pressure is placed on the rate of price inflation. For example, if the value of the United States dollar declines, it will cost Americans more to purchase Japanese TVs or Canadian raw materials. There is also a secondary effect in that a weak American dollar by definition puts more money into the hands of foreigners since their currencies can now buy more United States goods. If these claims are exercised, it increases the demand for such goods and has the effect, other things being equal, of raising their prices. Given the relationship between interest rates and inflation discussed earlier, it can be seen how the inflationary consequences of a declining currency have the effect of raising interest rates.

A declining currency also encourages investors and businesspeople to borrow heavily. The process works in the following way. Investors may believe that the currency will continue to lose value. If they have a position in the stockmarket of that country which they wish to maintain, they will probably borrow an amount equivalent to their equity position and convert the proceeds of the loan into a stronger currency. In that way they can still make a capital gain in the stock market with little or no currency risk. Similarly businesspeople who had made a sale of an asset or other item denominated in the weak currency might not be in a position to receive the money until some future date. In this case they would be advised to borrow an amount equivalent to the value of the sale and immediately convert the proceeds into a harder currency. In some cases there may be no economic reason for the borrowing other than the belief on the part of a large investor or speculator that the weak currency will continue to depreciate. Until closed out, these types of transactions put upward pressure on interest rates for two reasons: (1) By temporarily increasing the supply of currency for sale they push the value of the currency down still farther, which exacerbates the inflationary effect of a depreciating currency. (2) The borrowing process increases the demand for credit and therefore drains liquidity from the depreciating country's financial system, thus raising interest rates.

The basic reason for the declining currency in the first place is monetary and fiscal overstimulation working through to a robust economic recovery and current account deterioration. Consequently unless other governments outinflate the government of the depreciating currency, the latter will be forced into monetary tightening moves to cool its economy and correct its current account imbalance. In effect this was the position the United States government was forced into in October 1978, following a long period of dollar weakness. Currency markets therefore act as a discipline on governments that are, relatively speaking, overstimulating their economies in relation to their trading partners.

THE CAPITAL ACCOUNT

The capital account of the balance of payments is concerned with flows of investment capital from one country to another. The trend in the capital account can also have an important effect on interest rates. Since the overall balance of payments must by definition balance, the capital account is where the residue from the current account surplus or deficit is made up, either from private transactions or through central bank operations. If it were possible to construct a balance of payments for an individual, the current account would be made up of earnings, representing exports, and spending, representing imports. If earnings outstripped spending there would be a surplus, which would be saved. In effect the result would be exporting capital. On the other hand if spending outstripped earnings, the current account deficit would have to be financed either by drawing on savings or from a loan of some kind. Just as there is a limit on how far an individual can continue to run current deficit, so there is a limit to that of a country. For a country, however, it is possible to postpone the day of reckoning up to a point. For example, the United States ran a current account deficit throughout the 1960s but it was not until the 1970s that the United States dollar began its sharp slide on the world currency market as the world lost confidence in the ability of the United States to correct its current account imbalance.

In its simplest form the capital account may be divided into two sectors: private and official transactions. Private transactions consist basically of investment flows either for financial investments or for real assets. At the margin it is the demand for financial investments that are important. If a country is running a large current account deficit, it is possible to offset this outflow with an inflow of capital. However, in order to attract the required capital it will be necessary for the importing country to structure its interest rates at a level high enough relative to other countries to make the obvious currency risk attractive. From the other point of view it will also be attractive for corporations or governments of the depreciating currency to borrow money denominated in foreign currencies if foreign interest rates are low enough to offset any perceived deterioration in the weak currency. It will also be necessary for a country to pay a high rate of interest if investors are concerned with the threat of political instability or of capital or exchange controls that would hinder or preclude an easy repatriation of the invested money.

This has been a very simple and brief explanation of how external forces can influence the course of domestic interest rates. In a sense it is perhaps incorrect to use the term "external forces" since major swings in a country's current or capital accounts are determined as much by events at home as by those abroad. Consequently readers are advised to concentrate on the domestic forces affecting trends in interest rates, using the material covered in this chapter as a useful background.

SUMMARY

1. The interaction of domestic and external developments is an important influence on the level and trend of interest rates.

2. To some extent or another all countries are tied to the global interest-rate cycle. If one country's level of interest rates becomes too low in relation to that in the rest of the world, in the absence of any other countervailing factors, capital will flow into those countries offering a higher rate of return, thereby draining liquidity from the low-interest-rate country and forcing up its interest-rate structure.

3. A weak currency adversely affects the domestic trend of interest rates because it increases inflationary pressures and draws liquidity out of the financial system.

4. A strong currency has a favorable effect on the trend of interest rates because it has a depressing effect on the rate of price inflation and encourages liquidity to flow into the country.

12
INTEREST RATES AND TECHNICAL ANALYSIS

While previous chapters have dealt with the factors affecting interest-rate trends, this chapter is concerned with analyzing the trends themselves. Technical analysis is concerned with studying the action of the interest-rate market itself. It is important to incorporate this trend analysis into the overall approach because of the confusing inflationary and deflationary crosscurrents that develop at cyclical turning points. If the analysis were confined solely to a study of fundamental factors, it would increase the chances of a miscalculation because many financial and economic indicators have differing leads during each cycle and are not easy to quantify for timing purposes. An assessment of the fundamental factors therefore becomes a subjective process, so that there is always the possibility that a particular sector or new institutional development might have been overlooked or overemphasized. As a result the interest-rate peak or trough might arrive earlier or later than the facts at the time would seem to suggest. While fundamental analysis is useful from the point of view of telling us that sufficient economic and financial slack has developed to be consistent with an interest-rate peak and vice versa, technical analysis gives us the specific signal that these forces have reversed enough to actually change the trend of interest rates. Technical analysis is not therefore considered here as an end in itself but as an important adjunct to the main part of the analysis.

TREND DETERMINATION

PRICE PATTERNS

All financial markets move in trends, up, down, or horizontal. This is shown graphically in Figure 12-1 for an interest rate peak. Normally cyclical trends in interest rates do not reverse immediately from up to down, but are separated by a period during which their level moves sideways within a trading range. This is a transition period, in which tremendous inflationary and deflationary crosscurrents are taking place. Eventually one side or the other wins, and a new trend is set in motion. This type of price action is shown in Figure 12-2a. Quite often this battle will develop within two very clearly definable boundaries, as shown in Figure 12-2b, or will take the form of a less controlled environment. Over the years technicians concerned with the equity market have noted that these reversal areas can be categorized into a number of different formations or price patterns. Such price patterns are applicable to interest rates and bond prices as well. The formation illustrated in Figure 12-2 is known as a *rectangle.* The battle between borrowers and lenders is confined between two distinct parallel boundaries and is essentially in balance until one side or the other wins. This point is signalled by the *breakout,* following which it is normally safe to assume that a new trend has begun. When the breakout occurs in the direction opposite the previous trend, the pattern is known as a *reversal pattern.* When it occurs in the same direction as the previous trend, the pattern becomes one of *consolidation* or *continuation.* Figure 12-3 shows a

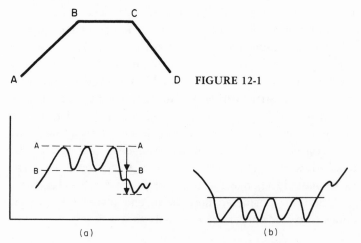

FIGURE 12-1

(a)   (b)   FIGURE 12-2

FIGURE 12-3

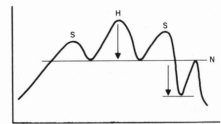

FIGURE 12-4

consolidation rectangle. A rectangle can occur at the top of the interest rate cycle or the bottom just before rates rise.

Space does not permit a full discussion of the various types of price patterns, and the description below is necessarily brief. For further study the reader is referred to the bibliography, where several stock market books, which are also applicable to the debt market in this sense, are listed.

The Head-and-Shoulders Pattern   A *head-and-shoulders* pattern consists of a head (the final rally) separated by two smaller rallies (the left and right shoulders). The right shoulder is in effect the first rally of a declining trend. The signal is given when interest rates break below the line joining the base of the two shoulders (known as the *neckline*). This is shown in Figure 12-4. At interest-rate troughs the same type of pattern is turned upside down, so to speak, and is known as an *inverse head and shoulders* (Figure 12-5). Again the reversal signal is given on the breakout above the neckline. The examples in Figures 12-4 and 12-5 have horizontal necklines, but such formations can also develop from rising or falling lines, as shown in Figure 12-6. These price patterns are still valid as long as the head protrudes beyond the two shoulders.

Head-and-shoulders formations can also be of the consolidation or continuation type, as shown in Chart 12-1, which shows the sharp bear market in bonds that began in 1977. In this chart bond prices, as opposed

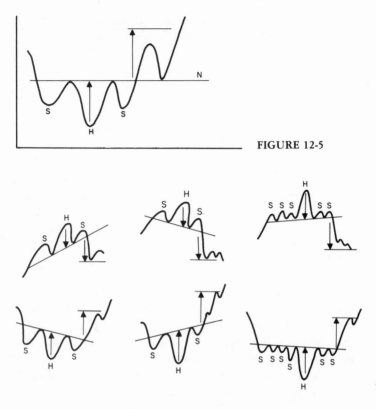

FIGURE 12-5

FIGURE 12-6

to actual interest rates, have been plotted. The break below the neckline provided a powerful signal of the carnage that was about to take place.

Sometimes a head-and-shoulders pattern appears to be forming, or actually is formed and then prices or interest rates reverse direction and continue their previous trend. Such situations where a head and shoulders does not work usually indicate that a final move in the prevailing trend is about to take place. Such a move is usually very sharp and dynamic. In rising markets it often represents the final blowoff stage: in an inverted head-and-shoulders failure, the resulting decline represents a final sharp decline. Such failures are rare, but when they do occur, they should be treated with the utmost respect.

Double Tops and Bottoms A *double-top* formation is essentially two rallies separated by a reaction and a subsequent decline below the reaction low. An example of a double top is shown in Figure 12-7. The reversal signal

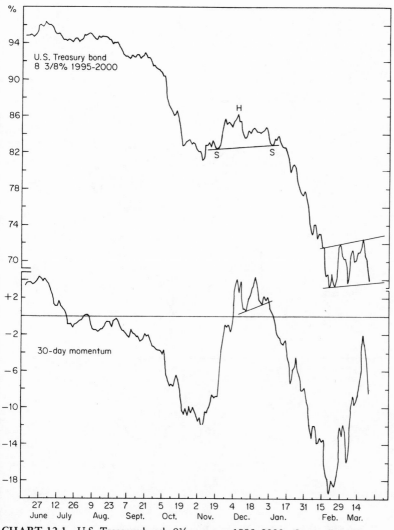

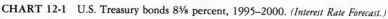

CHART 12-1   U.S. Treasury bonds 8⅜ percent, 1995–2000. *(Interest Rate Forecast.)*

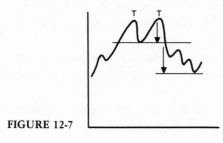

FIGURE 12-7

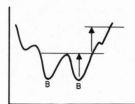

FIGURE 12-8

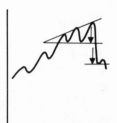

FIGURE 12-9

FIGURE 12-10

is given when the interest rate moves below the valley separating the two peaks.

A *double bottom* (Figure 12-8) is really the opposite of a double top. A signal is given when the interest rate moves above the peak in the rally separating the two bottoms.

The discussion above covered most of the important price patterns, but others are shown in Figures 12-9 to 12-12, giving their price objectives and breakout points.

Before leaving price patterns we should mention some general principles that help establish their significance:

1. The importance of a pattern is a consequence of its size. The longer a price pattern takes to complete and the greater its depth, that is, the degree of price fluctuation between the high and low point of the formation, the greater its significance. For example a head and shoulders that only takes 2 weeks to complete is unlikely to signal a cyclical peak in interest rates—in contrast to one that is formed over a longer period, of 3 months or more. This is because the longer pattern indicates that a very significant battle has taken place between borrowers and lenders. Consequently when one side is able to overcome the other, the event is of considerable importance.

2. Most tools used in technical analysis indicate the direction of prices not the magnitude of the swing. With price patterns it is possible to derive certain measuring functions. Such price objectives are only a guide and normally extend much farther than indicated. The measuring implications for rectangles, both head-and-shoulder varieties and double tops and bottoms, are calculated by measuring the depth of the patterns and projecting the vertical distance down or up, depending on the type of reversal. The measuring implication for a rectangle is shown in Figure 12-2. Measuring implications for other patterns are also illustrated.

3. It has so far been assumed that any breakout from a price pattern, however small, constitutes a valid signal of a trend reversal (or a resumption if the pattern is one of consolidation). Since misleading moves known as *whipsaws* occasionally develop, it is important to set up certain criteria in order to minimize such misrepresentations of the genuine trend or filter them out.

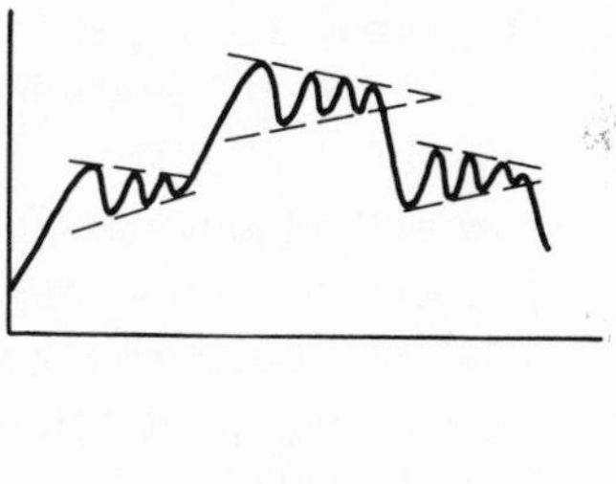

FIGURE 12-11

FIGURE 12-12

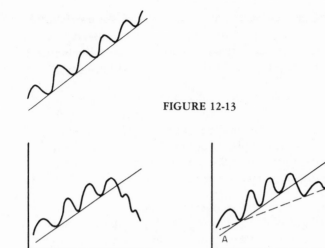

FIGURE 12-13

FIGURE 12-14

As a result it has been found more helpful to await a 3 percent penetration of the boundaries of the price formations before concluding that the breakout is indeed valid. While such signals will be less timely, this procedure usually filters out a substantial number of misleading moves and therefore results in a far more reliable procedure.

TRENDLINES

Close observation of any interest rate or bond trend indicates that in a rising phase it is often possible to join the bottoms of succeeding troughs with a line known as a *trendline* (Figure 12-13). When the interest rate falls below a trendline, the implication is either that a reversal in the trend has taken place or that a period of consolidation will develop as a temporary interruption of the prevailing trend. A new but less sharp trend will therefore result.

Figure 12-14 illustrates these two possibilities. Unfortunately there is no way of knowing at the time whether the trendline break indicates an actual reversal or a temporary interruption of the main trend. Normally it is possible to gain a clue from some of the principles governing trendline analysis discussed below or by reference to the maturity of the bull or bear market in interest rates derived from fundamental analysis.

If the break proves to be a temporary interruption of the main trend, a new trendline is drawn from the low point of the overall movement to the bottom of the most recent reaction whenever the interest rate in question achieves a new cyclical high. This is represented by the dashed line in Figure 12-14.

During interest-rate declines the reverse procedure holds, but in this case a trendline is drawn joining the declining series of peaks (Figure 12-15).

Sometimes a trendline break develops at the same time as a breakout from a price pattern, in which case it is fairly certain that the break is of the reversal type (see Figures 12-16 to 12-18). As with price patterns, trendline breaks can also indicate the possible magnitude of a move. The potential is obtained by finding the vertical distance between the highest peak (in a rising trend) and the trendline at that particular point and projecting that vertical distance downward at the juncture where the trendline is violated. Figure 12-19 indicates some of these possibilities for both rising and falling trends.

Three features of trendlines are important.

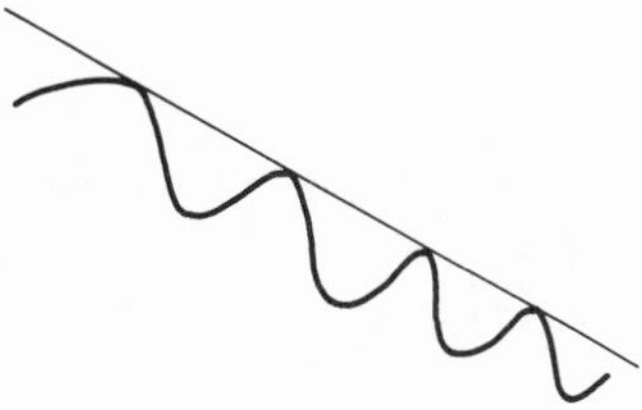

FIGURE 12-15

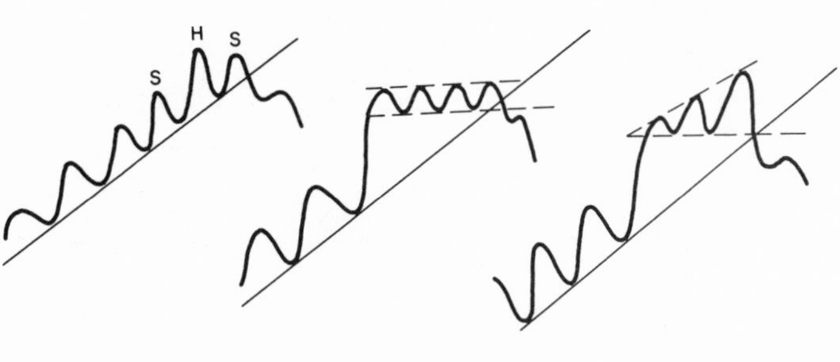

FIGURE 12-16

The Number of Times a Trendline Has Been Touched   Since a trendline is a relatively simple technique for identifying a price trend, it follows that the more times it has been touched, the more likely it is to represent a true reflection of that trend. Violation of a line that has been touched three or four times is therefore of far greater significance than one that has been touched only twice.

Steepness   Normally the steeper the slope of a trendline the less sustainable the trend it is identifying is likely to be. Consequently the violation of a steep trendline does not carry the same significance as one with a more gentle slope. Such penetrations tend to be of the continuation rather than the reversal type.

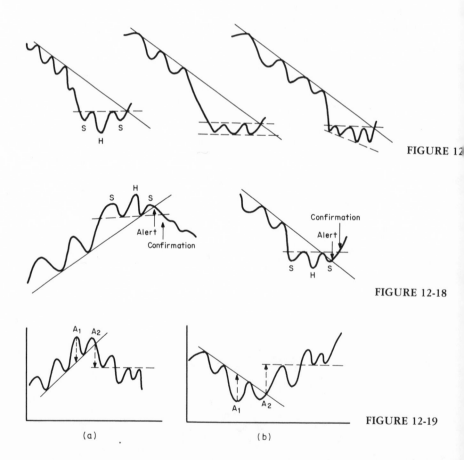

FIGURE 12

FIGURE 12-18

FIGURE 12-19

(a)   (b)

Length   Generally speaking, the longer and greater a price or interest-rate movement has been in force the longer and greater the corresponding trend in the opposite direction is likely to be. Since a trendline identifies the length of a trend, it follows that the significance of its penetration will be a direct function of its length. A violation of a trendline that has been in force for 2 or 3 years is likely to indicate a reversal of cyclical proportion compared with one that violates a 3- or 4-month trend, which has far less significance.

MOVING AVERAGES

The construction of a moving average was discussed in Chapter 8. The objective of a moving-average calculation in technical analysis is identical to that of trendline construction, namely, to isolate a price trend and find a reliable method of identifying its reversal at a relatively early stage. Changes in the direction of a trend are indicated when the price index or interest rate crosses above or below its moving average.

If the violation develops while the moving average is still proceeding in the direction of the prevailing trend, the possibility of a whipsaw exists and such a signal should be treated as a preliminary warning that a trend reversal has taken place. Confirmation can be given when the moving average itself changes direction, or it can be sought from some other technical source such as a breakdown from a price pattern or trendline.

On the other hand, if the moving average is flat or has already changed direction, its violation by the price index in question is normally a strong indication that the previous trend has been reversed.

Moving averages can be constructed to cover any time period, but the greater the span the longer the trend it is monitoring and therefore the greater the significance of its penetration.

Time spans which have proved to be the most useful historically have been 10 or 13 weeks for intermediate movements and 30 to 40 weeks for cyclical reversals.

RATE OF CHANGE OR MOMENTUM

A *rate-of-change index* calculates the rate at which a bond price or interest rate changes over a given period of time. To construct an index measuring a 12-month rate of change, for example, the current reading is divided by

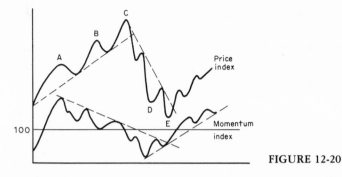

FIGURE 12-20

the reading 12 months ago. The subsequent reading is constructed by dividing next month's value by the value 11 months ago from today, that is, 12 months before next month's level. The result is then plotted as an oscillator which continually moves above or below a 100 reference line. When a plot occurs at the 100 level, it indicates that the current month's reading is exactly the same as it was 12 months ago. An index that never changed in price would therefore be plotted as a straight line along the 100 level.

When a rate-of-change index (sometimes referred to as a *momentum index*) is above the 100 reference line, the interest rate or bond price it is measuring is higher than the level with which it has been compared (in this case 12 months ago). If the momentum index is also rising, it is evident that the difference between the current reading and the level 12 months ago is growing. If the rate-of-change index is above the central line but is declining, the interest rate is still above its level 12 months ago but the difference is shrinking. The opposite is true when the line is below its 100 reference point.

In sum, a rising rate-of-change index implies growth in momentum, and a falling index implies a loss in momentum. Rising momentum should be interpreted as a bullish factor for bond prices (bearish for interest rates) and declining momentum as a bearish factor for bond prices (bullish for interest rates).

The momentum index is usually plotted below the bond price or interest rate it is measuring, as in Figure 12-20. Normally an interest rate will reach its maximum level of momentum reasonably close to the cyclical trough. In Figure 12-20 this is shown as point *A*. If the interest rate makes a new high which is confirmed by the rate-of-change index, no indication of technical weakness (in relation to the rising trend) arises. On the other hand, should the momentum index fail to confirm (point *B*), a negative divergence is set up between the two indexes and a warning of a possible reversal is given. Sometimes an interest rate will rally up to a third top, accompanied by even greater weakness in the momentum index. Alternatively the third peak in the momentum peak may be higher than the second but still lower than the first. In either case a distinct warning of a potential sharp reversal in the level of the interest rate is given. Whenever a divergence between momentum and the interest rate occurs, it is essential to wait for a confirmation from the interest rate itself that its trend has also been reversed. This confirmation can be given by (1) the violation of an important trendline, as shown in Figure 12-20, (2) the crossover of a moving average, or (3) the completion of a price pattern. This form of insurance is well worth it since during a long cyclical advance in rates, like that which developed between 1962 and 1966, it would not be unknown for a momentum index to lose and regain momentum continually without suffering a break in trend.

The same principles of divergence can also be applied to declining interest-rate trends. For example, in Figure 12-20 the interest rate makes a new low at point E, but the momentum index does not.

When the momentum index peaks simultaneously with price (as shown in Figure 12-21), no advance warning is given that a price decline is imminent. Nevertheless a clue indicating technical weakness is given when a trendline joining the troughs of the momentum index and the interest rate itself is penetrated on the downside.

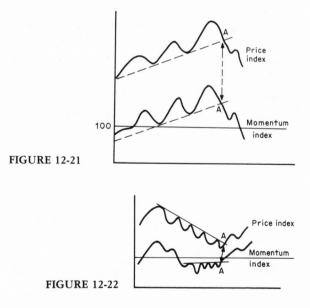

FIGURE 12-21

FIGURE 12-22

As with any trendline construction, judgment based on the principles outlined earlier is still required to determine the significance of the break. Moreover, the break in momentum should be regarded as an alert, and action should be taken only when it is confirmed by a break in the interest-rate trend itself (indicated by line AA in Figure 12-21).

Momentum indexes are also capable of tracing out price patterns. Consequently a breakout from a price pattern accompanied by a reversal in the downward trend of the interest rate or bond price itself is usually a highly reliable indication that a worthwhile move has just begun. Such an example is shown in Figure 12-22.

Another way momentum indexes can be useful relates to their level. Since this type of index is an oscillator fluctuating back and forth across its 0 or 100 reference line, there are clearly definable limits beyond which it rarely goes (see Figure 12-23).

The actual boundaries will depend on the volatility of the index being monitored and the length of time on which the rate of change is based, since the rate of change of an index has a tendency to vary more over a longer period than a shorter one.

In view of these two variables, there is no hard-and-fast rule saying what constitutes an unduly high or low level. This can be determined only with reference to the history of the interest rate or bond price being monitored and the maturity of the cycle. If we are considering bond prices when a bull market has just begun, for example, there is a far greater tendency for an index to move quickly into overbought territory and remain at very high readings for a considerable length of time. At such points the overbought readings tend to give premature warnings of declines. Consequently, during the early phases of the bull cycle, when the market possesses strong momentum, reactions to the oversold level are much more responsive to price reversals, and such readings therefore offer more reliable signals. It is only when the bull market is maturing or during bear phases that overbought levels indicate that a rally is shortly to be aborted. The fact that an index is unable to remain at such high readings for long is itself a signal that the bull market is losing momentum.

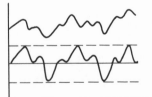

FIGURE 12-23

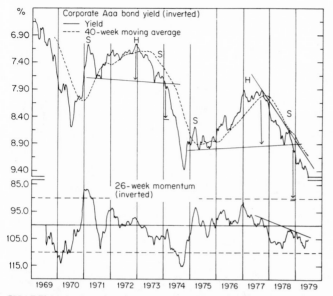

CHART 12-2 Moody's Aaa corporate bond yields plotted inversely to correspond with bond prices. Two head-and-shoulder distribution patterns developed between 1970 and 1973 and 1975 and 1978. When these inverted yields finally broke below their respective necklines, a substantial sell-off developed. In the case of the 1979–1980 experience, yields reached well in excess of 12 percent before a new bull market developed. *(Interest Rate Forecast.)*

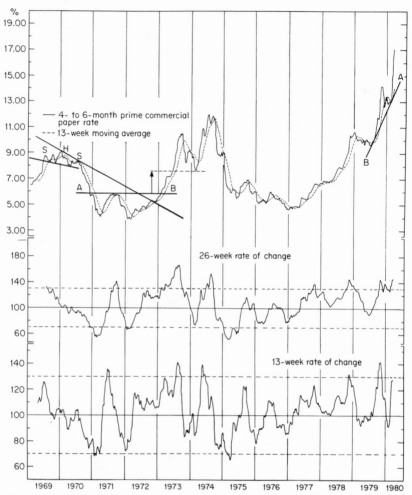

CHART 12-3 Four- to six-month commercial paper rate, 1969–1980, showing how the 1966–1969 bear market in short-term interest rates was terminated by a downward-sloping head-and-shoulder pattern. The 1972–1974 bear market, on the other hand, developed from a double bottom, the first occurring in early 1971 and the second at the beginning of 1972. A rise in rates above the dashed line *AB* was the signal that the double bottom had been completed. While the upside objective of about 7.9 percent was easily exceeded, this point proved to be the reversal point for the decline in late 1973 and early 1974. *(Interest Rate Forecast.)*

Charts 12-2 and 12-3 represent some actual examples in the marketplace of both price patterns and for extreme readings in momentum indexes. Note that whenever the 26-week rate of change index crosses above or below its extreme boundaries (marked by the dashed lines) and then returns within the confines of those boundaries, extremely strong 'buy' and 'sell' signals have resulted.

A further indication of the maturity of a trend is given when the momentum index moves strongly in one direction but the accompanying move in the price index is a much smaller one. Such a development suggests that the price or interest-rate index is tired of moving in the direction of the prevailing trend, for despite a strong push of energy from the momentum index, prices are unable to respond. This phenomenon is illustrated in Figure 12-24 at point *B* for both peaks and troughs.

PUTTING IT INTO PRACTICE

The charts included in this chapter demonstrate some examples of technical analysis. It is also useful to combine measures of momentum with a moving-average crossover to try to establish a more objective method of identifying trend reversals.

Chart 12-4 shows the weekly average of the federal funds rate with its 10-week moving average and its 13-week momentum. Whenever the rate itself crosses above its 10-week moving average and this is confirmed by the 13-week rate-of-change index moving above its 0 reference line, a signal that short-term interest rates are likely to move higher is given. A reversal in this trend can be signaled only when both the rate itself and the 13-week rate-of-change index cross below their respective reference levels again, namely, the 10-week moving average and the 0 reference line. A signal by one indicator is therefore not valid unless it is confirmed by the other. The shaded areas on Chart 12-4 represent periods when the Federal Funds Indicator is in a bearish position and unshaded areas when the indicator is in a bullish mode.

Reference to Chart 12-4 shows that when in force such signals usually last for some time although their record is far from perfect, as the whipsaw signals of 1970, 1979, and early 1980 show. Although the indicator does not suggest the magnitude of a move, it points up the likely climate for the debt markets as long as a specific signal is in force. Since most short-term rates are influenced by flow of funds rather than by expectations, the same type of approach could also be used for 4-month commercial paper

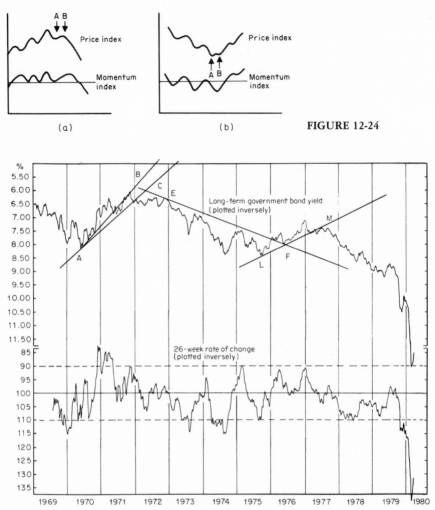

FIGURE 12-24

CHART 12-4 Long-term government bond yield index plotted inversely to correspond with bond prices. Trendline *AB* joined the 1970 cyclical low to the late 1970 reaction lows. It was violated in mid-1971, but even though this break turned out to be of the continuation rather than the reversal type, the extended line proved to be one of insurmountable resistance. On the other hand, a less steep trendline *AC* which joined the 1970 low to the mid-1971 lows did successfully signal the termination of the bull market.

Declining trendline *EF* extended over a 3-year period. It was relatively shallow and was touched four times. Its upward violation therefore proved to be of great significance as it signaled the termination of the 1972–1975 bear market for these bonds. Upward-sloping trendline *LM* was also characterized by a relatively shallow slope and was touched several times. It too signaled the end of a primary trend in yields. *(Interest Rate Forecast.)*

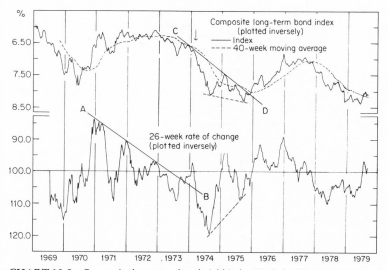

CHART 12-5   Composite long-term bond yield index (includes Moody's corporate Aaa bonds, Bond Buyer's 20 municipal bonds, St. Louis Federal Reserve long-term governments), showing two examples of momentum analysis. The index at the top of the chart is a composite long-term bond yield index constructed from yields of the three main bond market sectors, government, corporate, and tax-exempt. The index has been plotted inversely to correspond with bond prices. Since the upward violation of trendline *AB* of the 26-week rate-of-change index was not confirmed by a similar break in the yield index, a bullish signal was not forthcoming even though the momentum trendline was a relatively significant one. This example points out the need for a trend break in a momentum index to be confirmed by a similar one in the price or yield index it is measuring. The weakness of the technical position in late 1973 to early 1974 was also indicated by the fact that the yield index was actually declining in January 1974 in the face of strongly rising momentum. Note also the declining series of momentum peaks in 1970, 1971, and 1972 compared with the slightly rising series of highs in the yield index. These negative divergences were also pointing up the weakening technical structure.

In the fall of 1975 the technical position had improved since the 1975 low in the bond index was not confirmed by a new cyclical low in the rate-of-change index. This positive divergence (indicated by the dashed line) increased the bullish importance of the upward violation of trendline *CD* when it took place. *(Interest Rate Forecast.)*

but because of the more choppy yield action of long-term bonds mechanical systems are not recommended.

This type of system is very useful around major turning points even though its signals are usually of an intermediate proportion. If an assessment is made that most of the economic and financial indicators have given or are about to give an indication of a cyclical turning point, the technical system can greatly help in timing since this represents the first intermediate move in the new trend.

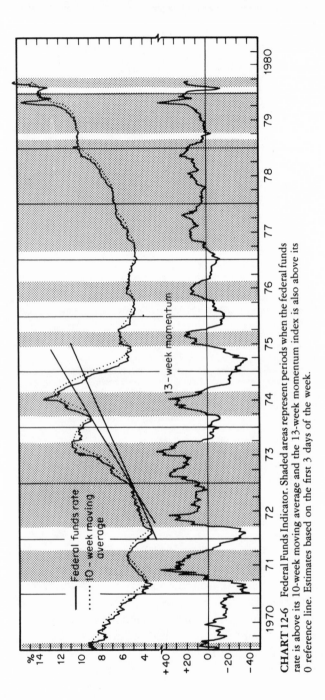

CHART 12-6 Federal Funds Indicator. Shaded areas represent periods when the federal funds rate is above its 10-week moving average and the 13-week momentum index is also above its 0 reference line. Estimates based on the first 3 days of the week.

160

13

SHORT-TERM INTEREST RATES DURING THE 1972–1974 INTEREST-RATE CYCLE

Having discussed the various factors affecting interest rates, we can now put them together in a way that will help to explain the 1972–1974 interest-rate cycle.

Short-term interest rates made their cyclical low in early 1972. At that time several economic and financial indicators had already bottomed out and had begun to move up, thereby pointing up the fact that the economy had begun to use up a considerable amount of economic and financial slack by this time. Chart 13-1 shows that the Composite Index of Lagging Indicators, the Help Wanted Index, and Commercial and Construction Contracts were all beginning to approach their 100 reference lines. The construction and interpretation of these indicators was discussed in Chapter 9. As reference to Chart 9-9 shows, interest-rate troughs have historically developed around the time these indicators bottomed out, so that the fact that they were closely approaching their trends indicated that time was running out for the bull market in short-term rates.

Growth in credit demands had also begun to show buoyancy, as can be seen in Chart 13-2, since each of the three series represented there had risen quite sharply from their late 1970 lows. The all loans all banks and commercial paper series in Chart 13-3 also crossed above its 96-month moving average, offering even more evidence that the cyclical expansion in the demand for credit was well under way.

At the time of the interest-rate low therefore, there was some fairly strong evidence that the stage was set for an interest-rate trough. Within a few months of the actual lows some even more conclusive evidence began to surface.

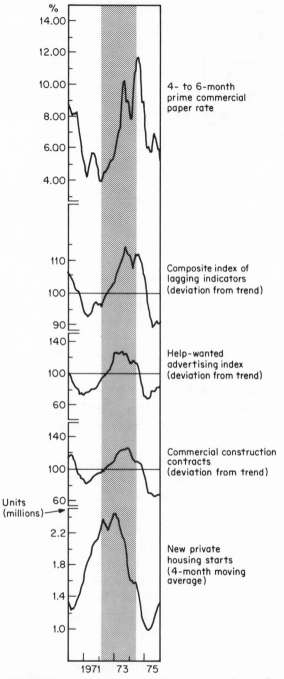

%
14.00
12.00
10.00
8.00
6.00
4.00

4- to 6-month
prime commercial
paper rate

110
100
90

Composite index of
lagging indicators
(deviation from trend)

140
100
60

Help-wanted
advertising index
(deviation from trend)

140
100
60

Commercial construction
contracts
(deviation from trend)

Units
(millions)

2.2
1.8
1.4
1.0

New private
housing starts
(4-month moving
average)

1971   73   75

CHART 13-1   Interest rates and the economy. *(Interest Rate Forecast.)*

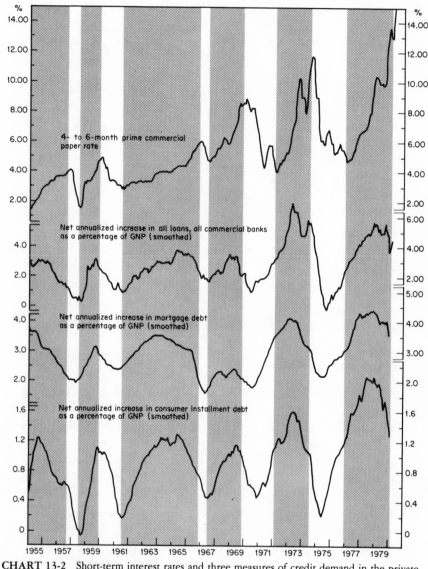

CHART 13-2 Short-term interest rates and three measures of credit demand in the private sector. *(Interest Rate Forecast.)*

The bank liquidity series in Chart 8-6, for instance, crossed above its 100 level, indicating a tightening of the banking system, not in the sense of actual tight money but as a hardening of the loan-deposit ratio in favor of loans. The Capacity Utilization Index also moved above its historical warning level of 82.5 in late 1972 (Chart 13-4).

Technically the interest-rate trend also looked as if it were making a

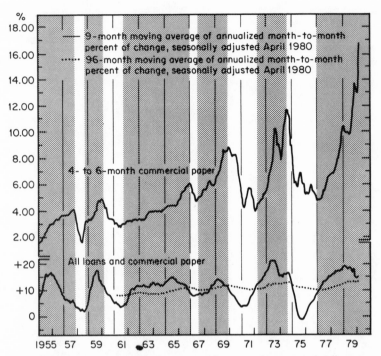

CHART 13-3 Four- to six-month commercial paper and loan growth (all commercial banks). *(Interest Rate Forecast.)*

reversal to the upside. For example, the trendline joining the mid-1970 top with the mid-1971 peak was violated on the up side shortly after the actual trough (see Chart 12-3). Confirmation of a double bottom was given as the 4- to 6-month yield moved above the mid-1971 peak (shown by the dashed line on Chart 12-3). Finally the Federal Funds Indicator, discussed on pages 157 and 159, gave a negative signal, indicating that the trend of interest rates was up. The Federal Reserve put the issue beyond doubt as it raised the discount rate from 4.5 to 5 percent in January 1973.

Rates continued their upward path until mid-1973. The following few months proved to be extremely confusing. First the pace of economic activity began to fall off, as illustrated by the indicators in Chart 13-1. Second, growth in the demand for credit as a percentage of the GNP (Chart 13-2) also peaked out. Third, the Federal Funds Indicator (Chart 12-6) gave a bullish signal, although it should be remembered that such signals are primarily intended as indications of intermediate trends.

At first sight it would have appeared at that time that rates had in fact peaked out. However, on a more conservative basis—and a conservative stance is usually the most sensible one to take—it could be noted that the

Capacity Utilization Index in Chart 13-4 was still at a relatively high level in excess of 85 percent, as was the Bank Liquidity Index (Chart 8-7). It would therefore take some time before these indicators could return to bullish readings. Also the Diffusion Index of Wholesale Prices, discussed on page 129, was still at a relatively high level, indicating that quite a lot of price inflation still had to work its way through the system. Another point worth noting is that short-term rates did not fall below long-term rates during this period, which would have been a powerful signal that easier credit conditions were likely to continue (see Chart 8-9). Finally, at no time during this confusing period between late 1973 and March of 1974 did the Federal Reserve indicate a return to an easy money policy by lowering the discount rate or reserve requirements.

The recession officially began in November 1973, but the virulent inflation that unfolded in the period from October 1973 to March 1974 caused a tremendous scramble for inventories as corporations perceived that they could make quicker profits in turning over inventories than in processing them for finished goods. While the growth of most other areas of credit demand continued their cyclical decline, the demand for loans to finance this inventory began to rise again, as discussed in Chapter 9. The scramble for commodities also had a modest effect on the economy. Reference to the indicators in Chart 13-1 shows either an upward blip or a temporary dissipation of the downward trend for many of them. At any rate, anyone who had jumped the gun in 1973 would have done well to pay attention to the Federal Funds Indicator (pages 157 and 160), which gave a bearish signal in March 1974 just as interest rates began to resume their sharp rise.

The peak in short-term rates occurred in the late summer and early fall

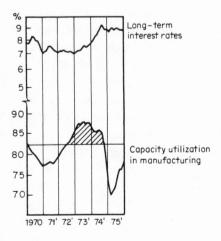

CHART 13-4 Long-term interest rates (Moody's Aaa corporates) and capacity utilization in manufacturing. *(Interest Rate Forecast.)*

of 1974 and was followed by a very steep decline. However, with the experience of the previous year's whipsaw still fresh, it would not have been prudent for conservative investors and businesspeople to have done anything but wait for some concrete signals. In retrospect it was quite easy to see not only that the recession had begun to bite but also that the involuntary inventory stage had been completed and that the temporary escalation in loan demand associated with this process was in the process of completion (see Chapter 9). Since these factors were not so evident at the time, one should therefore have proceeded more cautiously.

The evidence did not really become conclusive until late 1974. The first bullish development occurred around late September and early October. At this time the Federal Funds Indicator (pp. 157–160) gave a bullish signal while the trendline joining the 1972 and 1974 lows of the federal funds rate was violated on the down side (Chart 12-6). The cyclical trendline itself was much flatter and was violated in late 1974 (see Chart 12-6).

By November 1974 it was becoming clear that the rush for credit was over since the monthly average of 4- to 6-month commercial paper yield fell below that of AAA corporate yields for the first time since mid-1973. This latter signal still occurred early enough for participation in the ensuing bull market for bonds which had begun several weeks earlier.

The economic indicators were also moving into a position where it would have been safe to conclude that a cyclical interest rate peak had been seen. The 4-month moving average of Housing Starts had fallen to 1.2 million in December 1974, a level that had been associated with falling interest rates during the postwar period. The Help Wanted Index, perhaps the most reliable of the economic indicators, fell below its trend in the November-October period. The Capacity Utilization Index also fell very sharply in late 1974, well below its traditional 85 percent warning level. The Fed itself, concerned about economic overkill, put the issue more or less beyond doubt as it lowered the discount rate in December 1974.

While the Liquidity Index (Chart 8-6) did not turn bullish until early 1975, the technical, economic, and financial evidence left little doubt that considerable economic and financial slack was building up. One could proceed relatively confidently on the basis that the cyclical trend of interest rates at both the short and long ends was a downward one.

This brief outline of the 1972–1974 cycle has helped show that it is almost impossible to pinpoint cyclical turning points in the interest-rate cycle with any degree of accuracy or reliability based on the mechanical action of any one indicator. Forecasting interest-rate trends is therefore an art. The procedure involves the construction of many different indicators and the use of judgment in the assessment of each in relation to the individual business cycle being considered. It is not possible to follow one indicator slavishly because the characteristics of business cycles are different, both because of institutional changes and because one economic group invariably gets hurt more than the others during a recession and does not normally make the same mistake in succeeding cycles to the same degree. Also the economic importance of government, business, consumers, and the foreign sector changes over the years.

The only consistently successful approach to forecasting interest-rate trends and implementing the appropriate strategy is a conservative one since one cannot hope to identify each peak and trough as they occur. The most realistic consistently obtainable objective is the identification of a peak or trough area after the reversal has taken place. In this way it is possible to establish what the overall financial climate is likely to be and use this knowledge to take the appropriate action. This approach will also minimize the kind of unpleasant surprise that greeted most investors in the turbulent period of 1978–1979 when it was the (premature) belief of many that interest rates had peaked.

14
SUPPLEMENTARY CHECKLIST FOR SPOTTING INTEREST-RATE PEAKS AND TROUGHS

Since spotting interest-rate peaks and troughs can be a tricky business at best, here is a checklist of areas that can be monitored once the economic and financial indicators discussed in previous chapters have moved into the positions that have historically been consistent with cyclical reversals in interest rates.

INTEREST-RATE PEAKS

1. Look for a blowoff phase in the commodity markets and the subsequent sharp collapse in prices. This development underscores the fact that the economy has already entered the recessionary phase or is just about to. This was the case in March 1974 (short rates peaked in July and August) and in the spring of 1980, when the lead time between the commodity and interest-rate peak was almost nonexistent.

2. Look for some bankruptcies, especially in financial institutions. Such failures not only indicate a softening in business conditions but also alert the authorities to the fact that it is probably time to ease monetary policy or risk overkill. In 1970 Penn Central went bankrupt just at the time of the bond market bottom. The IOS scramble also occurred around the time of the cyclical peak. In 1980 it was the Hunt brothers' silver fiasco and the Pennsylvania National Bank that were in trouble close to the bear market low in bonds.

3. Sometimes the year-over-year rate of consumer price inflation

lags the peak in interest rates and therefore gives a belated signal, but normally even a lagging reversal in the trend develops soon enough to permit investors to participate in the bulk of the bull market in bonds.

4. Often a deeply oversold technical position, as measured by a rate of change in bond prices, will correspond with a peak in interest rates (see Chapter 12).

5. Sometimes a sharply falling currency will cause the authorities to tighten up more than necessary according to purely domestic economic factors. Interest rates therefore rise very sharply as a result of the authorities' reaction to the crisis, but a peak is usually seen within a few weeks or less. Such was the case in the United Kingdom in October 1976 (Chapter 11).

6. A panic selloff in the stock market following a long equity bear market often acts as a confirmation that an interest-rate peak is at hand or has just been seen. The reason is that the stock market is smelling out a sharp reduction in business activity consistent with falling interest rates. In June 1970 long rates peaked 1 month after a panic selloff in the stock market. Similarly the September-October 1974 bear market selling climax developed between the peaks in the short and long ends of the debt market.

7. Often it is time to buy bonds when the authorities openly decide that of the twin enemies, inflation and unemployment, greater emphasis should now be put on inflation. The Ford administration in late 1974 began its Beat Inflation Now campaign right at the time of peak rates of inflation and interest rates. The Carter administration also decided on a major monetary package and a strategy of balancing the federal budget right at the 1980 interest-rate peak. This was close to the peak in price inflation for that cycle (Chapter 7).

8. The first decline in the discount rate following several months or even years of hikes is a fairly safe confirmation that an interest-rate peak has been seen (Chapter 6).

9. At interest-rate peaks forecasts of wildly higher rates, typically by people who have incorrectly called peaks earlier in the cycle, are prevalent. Such predictions are often coupled with the implication that the long end of the bond market can never function properly again due to the greater volatility and uncertainty.

10. Interest-rate peaks are usually extremely volatile, with both short and long rates fluctuating in huge trading bands.

INTEREST-RATE TROUGHS

1. Interest-rate troughs are usually preceded by a pickup in business conditions; so look for a bottoming out and recovery in the commodity markets following a long and/or sharp decline.

2. The year-over-year rate of consumer price inflation will also have bottomed out and begun to turn up.

3. Following a long decline economic indicators such as Housing Starts and Help Wanted Advertising will have been rising for several months. Loan growth will also have begun to pick up. The Manufacturing Capacity Utilization Index will be close to, or higher than, 82.5 percent.

4. The technical condition will usually indicate a reversal of an important trendline or a major negative divergence with a long-term rate-of-change index (Chapter 12).

5. The stock market will have been rising for 9 months to 2 years. This again is a confirmation that a business recovery is well under way and that the economic slack resulting from the recession has begun to be used up.

6. The money supply, reflecting both easy money policies and increased credit demands, will have begun to move above official targets, therefore requiring the adoption of some credit-tightening procedures by the Fed (Chapter 6).

7. Following a long series of declines, the Fed raises the discount rate. This normally confirms the rise that has already taken place in short-term rates as a genuine cyclical movement, since for political reasons the Fed usually follows rather than leads rates upward at the early stage of the bear market in debt markets (Chapters 6 and 7).

8. If the external value of the dollar has been falling long enough for there to be a considerable lack of confidence in the United States monetary authorities, this will probably precipitate a tighter monetary policy.

9. If the administration and Congress begin to feel pressure for a tax cut due to high unemployment levels and the justification

can be rationalized through a trend toward lower price inflation rates, interest rates are probably ready to move up. The
aborted Carter tax cut proposal of 1976 falls into this category,
for by the time Congress got round to considering such legisla-
tion it was realized that the recovery was well under way and
the cut was unnecessary.

10. In contrast to the violent movements of short-term interest
rates and bond prices at interest-rate peaks, interest-rate
troughs are usually very dull affairs with comparatively little
price movement. As the interest-rate trough develops, rates
begin to move up faster and faster, so that the trough period
has the tendency to become rounded.

15

INTEREST-RATE FORECASTING: SOME PRACTICAL APPLICATIONS

It is clear that forecasting the trend of interest rates and identifying cyclical turning points is relatively easy if you are prepared to accept the fact that it is more or less impossible to pick the exact top and bottom with any degree of consistency.

If investors or businesspeople adopt some of the strategies discussed in this chapter, they should do so with the full knowledge that they are likely to miss the actual turning point by a month or so; but they have the security of knowing that they are likely to participate in most of the cyclical trend. Since volatility has replaced stability as the basic economic environment, this more conservative attitude can still offer substantial profits or ensure against undue risk.

There are basically two strategies that can be adopted if you believe a major reversal in the trend of interest rates is under way. The first is concerned with a change in the maturity of the portfolio of debt assets held or liabilities that have been incurred, depending on whether you are a borrower or a lender. If you are a lender, for example, and you think that interest rates are going to rise, you are better off lending on a short-term basis and then converting these assets into long-term debt at around the interest-rate peak. In that way it is not only possible to lock in high interest rates for a long period but also to obtain some benefit from the rise in price of long-term debt securities that develops in an environment of falling interest rates.

As a borrower, on the other hand you should adopt a completely different strategy. If you feel that rates are headed higher, you are better off taking advantage of the lower interest rates and borrowing for a long period of time right away.

The second type of strategy occurs where it is not possible or practical to change the maturity structure of a portfolio or restructure liabilities to take advantage of a change in the level of interest rates. In such cases the technique of hedging the position can be used. For example, having sold a house and taken back a mortgage, you may feel that interest rates are going to fall. If this proves to be the case, you will benefit in the sense that you have locked in the high yield on the mortgage for a long period of time. On the other hand, since the market for individual mortgages is so illiquid you would not be able to take full advantage of the appreciation in bond prices. You would therefore be advised to hedge your mortgage position by buying long-term Treasury or Government National Mortgage futures. In this particular case a relatively risk-free strategy could only be implemented if the outstanding value and maturity of the mortgage could be fairly closely matched with that of the short futures position, and if the spread between the far-out contracts were not too much out of line with those of the cash market.

With these two possible strategies in mind the following discussions represent some practical applications.

MORTGAGE STRATEGIES FOR INDIVIDUALS

It is not always possible to time the purchase or sale of a property to suit a particular stage in the interest-rate cycle, but once a firm opinion of the future course of interest rates has been established, this knowledge should be used to structure the maturity of a mortgage.

For example, the prospective purchaser of a property who believed that an interest-rate peak was at hand or had just occurred would be well advised to take out a 1-, 2-, or even 3-year mortgage and refinance the property on a longer-term basis at a lower rate of interest when the short-term mortgage matured. Since it is almost impossible to tell how long the declining phase of the interest-rate cycle is likely to last, an alternative method would be to finance the property purchased with a variable-rate mortgage. When the purchaser felt that rates were actually at their trough, the property could be refinanced on a fixed-rate basis but over a relatively long time. Of course it would be necessary to check that such refinancing was permitted under the mortgage agreement. Usually this is possible on payment of a penalty or bonus, but even when this charge is spread over the life of a mortgage, it is normally still a worthwhile proposition.

If you are a vendor, it is obviously inadvisable to take back a long-term mortgage when interest rates are at or around their lows, since you will be locked into receiving a very low interest rate well below forthcoming market levels. You could always sell the mortgage, but the discount from face value would be large due to the illiquidity of such investments. In any event, since money is usually readily available from lending institutions when interest rates are at their cyclical lows, the purchaser should have no trouble in raising the necessary money. A purchaser unable to acquire financing during such periods would probably be a bad risk anyway.

INVESTORS

In principle, investors with a large portfolio of debt securities should shorten the maturity of the portfolio when they feel interest rates will rise and lengthen maturities when they consider that an interest-rate peak has been seen. However, there is a drawback to this strategy at the beginning of the cycle when rates are at their trough; there is often a considerable loss of income since short rates are usually well below long ones at this cyclical juncture. As an investor you are therefore faced with the dilemma of trading off the preservation of the capital value of your portfolio with this income loss. If income is not a problem, this will not prove to be an insurmountable difficulty. On the other hand, if it is, you may well be advised to continue holding your bonds but selling long-term interest-rate futures contracts against all or part of your holdings. In this way you will not only be able to maintain the income from the bonds but will also preserve the capital value of your overall portfolio, for theoretically the loss on your bond holdings should more or less be offset by a profit from the short position. While this strategy sounds simple in theory, it is not always so easy to put into practice since the futures markets will usually discount some of the expected rise in interest rates. Consequently the price of the deferred or far-out contracts might be considerably below that of the cash market. Over the period of a rising cyclical interest-rate trend one or two points will not make too much difference and are well worth paying as insurance. On the other hand, if the spread between the cash price and the far-out contracts is 4 to 6 points, the market has clearly gone a long way toward discounting the interest-rate rise and far greater caution will be required in taking on this hedge.

Another situation in which hedging should be considered as a possible strategy to combat rising interest rates occurs if you are an investor in a high tax bracket looking for tax-free income. Since it is very difficult to obtain tax-exempt securities with a short-term maturity, as a tax-exempt-oriented investor you are more or less forced to hold onto your long-term tax-exempt bonds or suffer the consequences of a short-term taxable yield. If you were to short long-term futures against your tax-exempt position, you could maintain the value of your portfolio by offsetting the unrealized loss on your long position with the profit on the short side. Such a situation would not be totally to your advantage since you would be subject to short-term gains tax when the profits from the short sale were realized. Even so, this strategy would still protect you from a large part of the potential capital loss on your tax-exempt bonds so that you could use the tax-free portion of your short-sale gain to buy more tax-exempt bonds at around their bear market lows, further augmenting your income.

At the top of the interest-rate cycle the opposite strategies are appropriate in that investors should lengthen maturities. Normally at cyclical peaks short rates will be offering a more juicy yield than long rates, so again there is a trade-off between potential capital gain (from purchasing bonds) and income loss from giving up short-term debt instruments. This does not present anything like the dilemma faced during the trough period since short-term rates usually fall very sharply after they have reached their highs and do not normally remain above long rates for very long. Indeed the crossover point sometimes occurs when or immediately after bond prices have reached their lows. Reference to Chart 8-9 shows that this was the case at the 1959–1960, 1969–1970, and 1974 peaks. In 1953 and 1957 the problem did not arise since short rates never rose significantly above long rates at any time during the cycle.

BUSINESS

Corporations are faced with quite a dilemma when setting interest-rate policies because the periods when business is good and capital expenditure projects are being planned are usually the time when borrowing costs are highest. Similarly when interest rates are low, business is usually at or around its poorest, so that it does not appear at the time to make good sense to turn short-term loans, which are used to finance inventories, into long-term loans, which are difficult to pay off if business conditions worsen and lower inventory levels become more desirable. Moreover, there seems to be no urgency for such a move since short-term rates are well below those which would have to be paid for long-term debt. To convert short-term debt into long-term debt when interest rates are at their lowest would therefore involve higher borrowing costs initially.

In such a situation a corporation could adopt a hedging policy in that it continues to borrow the same amount of money on a short-term basis but at the same time shorts some GNMA or Treasury bond futures. If the far-out contracts were not selling at too much of a discount, that is, below current cash prices, the corporation would make a capital gain on its futures position as interest rates rose. When short-term rates began to approach long-term rates, the short position could be closed out and the short-term debt converted into long-term debt. In this way the corporation would have taken full advantage of its knowledge that interest rates were at or approaching their cyclical low. It is unlikely that it would convert all its short-term debt into a longer-term maturity since the corporation would still wish to retain some financial flexibility.

At interest-rate peaks, the strategy would be reversed in that a cash-hungry corporation would continue to finance as much of its debt as possible with bank loans and other short-term instruments. As interest rates fell, it would then convert the short-term debt into a longer maturity, thereby locking in the low yield. On the other hand, if the corporation felt that interest rates were going to fall but it was not in a position to maintain its financing at the short end due to general credit tightness, board policy, and the like, it could still take advantage of its knowledge through the purchase of long-term Treasury futures. The capital gain from the futures position would then partially offset the fact that it was forced to issue long-term debt near the cyclical interest-rate peak.

Businesspeople can also use their knowledge of the forces affecting interest-rate trends to forecast business conditions and therefore improve the timing of business decisions. For example, it is possible to tell from the liquidity and economic indicators that the economy has been in a recovery phase for some time and may soon overheat.

For businesses that are sensitive to economic conditions this is very important information to have and to act upon. If you believe that credit is soon going to be in tight supply, it would make sense to try to become as liquid as possible, to extend lines of credit, and, if possible, to convert variable-interest demand loans into longer-term bank loans with a fixed interest rate. In this way it will be possible to avoid many of the painful effects of the tight-credit stage of the business cycle. Part of the liquifying process might involve lowering inventory levels or postponing shorter-term capital projects, curtailing hiring, and so forth.

Once the interest-rate peak has been seen, it would be wise to extend the maturity of any money market instruments that has been built up during the period of reliquidification. Similarly once the economic indicators began to indicate that the economy has entered its initial stages of recovery, many capital projects previously postponed could be undertaken and long-term financing arranged at relatively low levels of interest rates.

EQUITY INVESTORS

Since declining interest rates are usually good for stocks, investors in the equity market can begin to consider reaccumulating their equity positions once they have established that an interest-rate peak has occurred. Normally interest-sensitive stocks, such as financial institutions and utilities, are the first groups to turn around and lead the new bull market higher. Preferred shares are also extremely sensitive to changes in interest rates, so they also tend to bottom out ahead of the rest of the stock market, except for specific issues where there is a serious risk of a cut in dividends.

The lead between interest-rate troughs and stock-market peaks has varied during this century from 1 or 2 months to as much as 3 years. However, since all equity bull market peaks since the turn of the century have been preceded by a trough in interest rates, a trend toward rising rates is clearly an important indication that the bull market is probably drawing toward its terminal phase. As an investor, once you have come to the conclusion that the cyclical trough in interest rates has been seen, you would normally be wise to begin a selling program of the more interest-sensitive groups, such as utilities, financial institutions, and certainly preferred shares. Occasionally fundamental factors other than interest rates can continue to have a favorable effect on these stocks, and so it is important for investors to check them out further so that the evidence can be weighed.

A strategy that margined stock investors can adopt if there is good reason for expecting their equities to rise even in the face of increasing interest rates is to try to arrange with their banker to freeze the rate of interest they are paying on their margin loan. Some bankers will agree to do this at a slightly higher rate than that prevailing at the time. They are also happy to do the business, for at this stage in the business cycle loan growth is at a relatively low level and the banks have lots of spare capacity.

ENTREPRENEURS

Another possibility for cashing in on interest-rate trends occurs just after the cyclical interest-rate peak. At this time short rates are either below long rates or are likely soon to fall below them. An enterprising person armed with the knowledge that rates generally are likely to fall for some considerable time can make money by borrowing short and lending long. For example, if you are able to borrow at 8 percent and lend long at 10 percent, it is possible to make a 2 percent spread per annum on your investment.

Some people like to buy mortgages for this purpose. Quite often, for example, the vendor of a house who takes back a first mortgage in order to make the house more salable will sell that mortgage at a discount to a mortgage broker or someone else. Since a private mortgage is a very illiquid debt instrument, the discount can be considerable: for example, if current rates are 10 percent, the mortgage might be discounted to yield 12 percent or more. The amount of the discount will depend upon such factors as the size of the purchaser's down payment and the age, condition, and location of the house. The point is that for anyone willing to take on the risk of a mortgage, it is possible to obtain a relatively high spread between the borrowed cost and the yield on the mortgage. The risk, apart from that of default on the mortgage itself and the cost of repossession, is that the declining cycle in interest rates is relatively short and that it might not be possible to redispose of the mortgage at a satisfactory price. On the assumption that the mortgage is a relatively short one of, for example, 5 years, one way around this problem is to borrow short against the mortgage following the interest-rate down. As it becomes apparent that the interest-rate cycle is beginning to reverse upward, try to freeze the interest rate on the short-term loan for 1 to 2 years, offering to pay your banker a slightly higher rate than you are already paying. The chances are that if you have a good relationship with your banker, he will go for the proposition since most bankers are very poorly informed on the subject of interest-rate forecasting.

If you do not like the idea of borrowing short against a mortgage, it is also possible to borrow short against a long-term bond. If the transaction is made close to the interest-rate peak, the difference in yield between the loan rate and the bond coupon will be relatively small, but as interest rates fall, your (borrowing) costs will decrease while the interest you receive stays the same. In addition of course, the price of the bond will go up, thereby contributing even greater profit to the transaction.

Normally for such transactions the bank might require you to put up a substantial amount of your own money into the long-term bond as security. However, it is possible to purchase federal government obligations, because of their high quality and liquidity, with as little as 10 to 15 percent margin. In this way you can obtain substantial leverage and will be able to make a considerable amount of money if your opinion proves to be correct. If your opinion proves to be incorrect, the leverage will work against you, so that it is a good idea for you to be very careful in terms of assessing both your financial condition and your view of the market before entering into such transactions.

CONCLUSION

The strategies discussed above are a few of the many possibilities that exist once you have a clear and well-reasoned approach to forecasting interest rates. Resourceful readers will undoubtedly be able to think of many more that might be applicable to their own situation.

The approach taken and the strategies discussed have been oriented to a business-cycle view of the interest-rate cycle. Normally this cycle will operate around a 3- to 5-year period, but sometimes its duration can be much shorter, as was the experience in 1966 and 1967, when the downward phase of interest rates lasted for only a few months. This example serves as a final warning that once you have correctly identified an interest-rate peak (or trough), it is not good practice to sit back and relax for a year or two. The forecasting process, while relatively simple when stripped down to its basics, is and must be a constant task if it is to be put into successful practice. Investors and businesspeople must also be continually on the watch for new institutional developments capable of distorting the indicators previously found most useful in the forecasting approach.

Finally, readers are cautioned against paying undue attention to the views of "experts" as quoted in the popular press. Normally when there is a concensus view relating to an interest-rate juncture point, this view proves to be fallacious. Readers are better advised to form their own independant judgment based on a concensus approach of the indicators rather than the concensus view of other people.

APPENDIX

This is a brief list of some of the official publications sponsored by the government and Federal Reserve Board that are useful for obtaining data for the construction of indicators together with background material.

Survey of Current Business

Department of Commerce, Superintendent of Documents, U.S. Government Printing Office, Washington DC 20402

Includes some articles but is mainly a source for economic statistics. Published monthly for an annual cost of about $25. Biennial supplements listing historical data for economic statistics are also published.

Business Conditions Digest

Department of Commerce, Superintendent of Documents, U.S. Government Printing Office, Washington DC 20402

Includes economic statistics and a wealth of excellent charts of important economic and financial indicators over a number of business cycles. The approximately $50 subscription for 12 monthly issues is well worth the investment. Supplements containing historical data are also published from time to time.

Federal Reserve Bulletin

The Board of Governors of the Federal Reserve System, Washington DC 20551

Approximate cost $20 per annum for 12 monthly issues. Includes articles but is mainly useful for its coverage of monetary data. Supplements containing historical data are also produced.

Federal Reserve Chart Book

Publications Services, Division of Support Services, Board of Governors of the Federal Reserve System, Washington DC 20551

Contains charts of economic and financial data over a 10-year period. The subscription price of $7 per annum includes four chart books plus a historical chart book which is issued once a year.

U.S. Financial Data Research Department

Federal Reserve Bank of St. Louis, P.O. Box 442, St. Louis, MO 63166

Published weekly, it contains key monetary data and charts. Subscription free on demand.

Federal Reserve Statistical Releases

The Federal Reserve issues a number of statistical releases on a monthly and/or weekly basis. It is not necessary to receive all these releases, but the following ones are useful from the point of view of constructing the liquidity indexes.

Statistical Release G.7

Contains important data concerning bank loans and securities held by banks (see Table A-1).

Statistical Release H.6

Reports important data concerning money supply and money-supply components (see Tables A-2 and A-3).

Other Sources

Economic and financial data are widely reported in the financial press. *The Wall Street Journal* and the business section of *The New York Times* offer the best up-to-date coverage. These two sources also reprint weekly statistics on money supply, loans, and other banking data as reported by the Federal Reserve each Friday afternoon.

TABLE A-1 Loans and Investments at All Commercial Banks, 1979 (Monthly average figures, billions of dollars)[a,b]

	Seasonally adjusted						Not seasonally adjusted					
	July	Aug	Sept	Oct	Nov	Dec	July	Aug	Sept	Oct	Nov	Dec
1. Total loans and securities[c]	1092.2	1102.8	1122.8	1128.9	1128.4	1131.5	1093.7	1102.7	1124.7	1130.9	1130.5	1141.7
2. U.S. Treasury securities	95.3	94.1	95.2	95.3	94.3	93.7	93.6	92.2	93.6	93.2	93.4	94.8
3. Other securities	183.5	185.4	187.6	188.8	190.5	191.6	183.3	185.0	187.6	189.0	190.7	192.4
4. Total loans and leases[c]	813.4	823.6	840.0	844.8	843.6	846.2	816.8	825.5	843.5	848.7	646.5	854.6
5. Commercial and industrial loans	275.5	279.9	285.9	288.6	288.3	289.8	276.9	279.6	285.8	288.4	288.3	291.8
6. Real estate loans[d]	228.7	231.3	234.1	237.1	239.7	242.4	228.9	232.0	235.3	238.3	240.9	242.9
7. Loans to individuals	177.8	178.8	180.2	181.3	182.3	NA	178.2	180.4	182.4	183.3	183.7	NA
8. Security loans	23.6	23.0	23.5	20.6	18.4	18.2	22.7	23.0	23.6	20.8	18.8	19.4
9. Loans to nonbank financial institutions	29.2	29.5	29.8	30.9	30.9	30.3	29.5	29.8	30.3	31.0	31.0	30.8
10. Agricultural loans	29.1	29.2	29.6	30.0	29.4	31.0	29.5	29.8	30.1	30.3	29.5	30.8
11. Lease financing receivables	8.3	8.6	8.7	8.9	9.1	9.4	8.3	8.6	8.7	8.9	9.1	9.4
12. All other loans	41.2	43.2	48.0	47.4	45.5	NA	42.8	42.3	47.2	47.6	45.2	NA

183

Memoranda (Table A-1, *Cont.*)

1. Total loans and investments plus loans sold[c-e]	1095.9	1106.5	1126.5	1132.5	1132.0	1134.5	1097.4	1106.4	1128.4	1134.5	1134.1	1144.5
2. Total loans plus loans sold[c-e]	817.2	827.0	843.7	848.4	847.2	849.0	820.5	829.2	847.2	852.3	850.1	857.4
3. Total loans sold to affiliates[c,e]	3.7	3.7	3.7	3.6	3.6	2.8	3.7	3.7	3.7	3.6	3.6	2.0
4. Commercial and industrial loans plus loans sold[c,e]	278.3	282.6	288.7	291.2	290.8	291.6	279.7	282.4	288.6	291.1	290.8	293.6
5. Commercial and industrial loans sold[e]	2.8	2.8	2.8	2.7	2.5	1.8	2.8	2.8	2.8	2.7	2.5	1.8
6. Acceptances held	8.2	8.0	8.6	8.0	7.6	7.9	7.9	7.5	8.0	7.9	7.9	8.8
7. Other commercial and industrial loans	267.3	271.8	277.3	280.6	280.7	282.0	269.1	272.1	277.8	280.5	280.4	283.0
8. To U.S. addressees[f]	250.0	253.7	258.7	261.1	261.3	263.2	251.7	254.2	259.2	261.4	260.9	263.2
9. To non-U.S. addressees[f]	17.3	18.1	18.6	19.5	19.4	18.8	17.3	17.9	18.7	19.2	19.5	19.8
10. Loans to foreign banks	20.9	20.9	24.0	22.9	19.4	18.6	21.9	20.6	23.6	22.4	18.9	20.1
11. Loans to commercial banks in the U.S.	68.8	70.9	75.9	76.4	75.0	77.8	65.6	66.4	73.5	74.2	76.4	81.9

[a] Data are prorated averages of Wednesday data for domestic chartered banks and averages of previous month-end data for foreign-related institutions. Back data are available from the Banking Section, Division of Research and Statistics.

[b] Includes domestic chartered banks, United States branches, agencies, and New York investment company subsidiaries of foreign banks and Edge Act corporations.

[c] Excludes loans to commercial banks in the United States.

[d] Loans sold are those sold outright to a bank's own foreign branches, nonconsolidated nonbank affiliates of the bank, the bank's holding company (if not a bank), and nonconsolidated nonbank subsidiaries of the holding company.

[e] As of Dec. 1, 1979, loans sold to affiliates and commercial and industrial loans sold were reduced $800 million and $700 million, respectively, due to corrections of two banks in New York City.

[f] The United States includes 50 states and the District of Columbia.

NA = not available.

SOURCE: *Federal Reserve Statistical Release G.7* (407), Jan. 22, 1980.

TABLE A-2 Money Stock Measures and Liquid Assets (Billions of dollars, seasonally adjusted unless otherwise noted)[a]

Year Month	M₁A — Currency plus demand deposits[b]	B₁B — M₁A plus other checkable deposits at banks and thrift institutions[c]	Addenda — Overnight RPs at commercial banks plus overnight Eurodollars[d], not seasonally adjusted	Addenda — Money market mutual fund shares, not seasonally adjusted	M₂ — M₁B plus overnight RPs and Eurodollars, MMMF shares, and savings and small time deposits at commercial banks and thrift institutions[e]	M₃ — M₂ plus large time deposits and term RPs at commercial banks and thrift institutions[f]	L — M₃ plus other liquid assets[f]
1979 Feb	350.0	360.7	23.6	14.5	1412.8	1640.2	1952.8
Mar	351.9	363.9	24.8	16.8	1425.4	1652.6	1976.0
Apr	356.2	369.7	25.1	19.2	1440.2	1666.5	1998.1
May	356.1	369.5	26.3	21.8	1448.3	1674.9	2016.7
June	360.3	374.3	26.0	24.6	1464.5	1689.5	2043.0
July	363.2	378.0	25.1	28.0	1476.4	1702.9	2057.3
Aug	365.4	380.7	25.2	31.2	1489.5	1719.3	2074.9
Sept	367.5	383.2	26.1	33.7	1499.7	1738.2	2103.3
Oct	368.0	383.9	25.6	36.9	1507.2	1751.8	2115.2
Nov	369.6	385.3	23.5	40.4	1514.5	1762.6	2124.2
Dec	371.5	387.7	24.1	43.6	1524.1	1773.5	2141.2
1980 Jan P	372.6	389.1	24.9	49.1	1532.7	1785.2	2156.4
Feb P	376.3	392.9	25.0	56.8	1546.7	1802.5	

Table A-2 (Cont.)

Week Ending:			
1980 Feb 6	377.2	393.7	24.4
13	376.3	392.8	23.2
20	377.6	394.1	26.3
27	374.6	391.1	25.2
Mar 5 P	374.6	391.4	25.9
12 P	376.3	393.3	23.5

[a] P = preliminary data. Special caution should be taken in interpreting week-to-week changes in money-supply data, which are often highly volatile and subject to revision in subsequent weeks and months. Preliminary data are subject to weekly revisions until they are final.

[b] Includes (1) demand deposits at all commercial banks other than those due to domestic banks, the United States government, and foreign banks and official institutions less cash items in the process of collection and Federal Reserve float and (2) currency outside the Treasury, Federal Reserve Banks, and the vaults of commercial banks.

[c] M_{1A} plus NOW and ATS accounts and banks and thrift institutions, Credit Union share-draft accounts, and demand deposits at mutual savings banks.

[d] Overnight and continuing-contract RPs are those issued by commercial banks to the nonbank public, and overnight Eurodollars are those issued by Caribbean branches of member banks to United States nonbank customers.

[e] Small time deposits are those issued in amounts of less than \$100,000. M_2 will differ from the sum of components presented in subsequent tables by a consolidation adjustment that has been made to avoid double counting of the public's monetary assets. The difference represents the amount of demand deposits held by thrift institutions at commercial banks.

[f] Large time deposits are those issued in amounts of \$100,000 or more and are net of the holdings of domestic banks, thrift institutions, the United States government, money market mutual funds, and foreign banks and official institutions. Term RPs are net of RPs held by money market mutual funds.

[g] Other liquid assets include the nonbank public's holdings of U.S. Savings Bonds, short-term Treasury securities, commercial paper, and bankers' acceptances net of money market mutual fund holdings of these assets.

SOURCE: *Federal Reserve Statistical Release H.6* (508), Mar. 21, 180.

TABLE A-3 Components of Money Stock Measures and Liquid Assets (Billions of dollars, seasonally adjusted unless otherwise noted)

Year Month	Currency^a	Demand deposits^b	Other checkable deposits^c, not seasonally adjusted	Overnight RPs net^d, not seasonally adjusted	Overnight Eurodollars^e, not seasonally adjusted	Money market mutual funds^f, not seasonally adjusted	Savings deposits			Small-denomination time deposits		
							At commercial banks	At thrift institutions	Total	At commercial banks	At thrift institutions	Total
1979 Feb	98.9	251.1	10.8	20.9	2.6	14.5	209.9	250.7	460.6	195.6	360.3	555.9
Mar	99.6	252.3	12.0	22.0	2.8	16.8	207.8	249.1	456.9	198.1	367.4	565.6
Apr	100.2	256.0	13.5	22.4	2.8	19.2	206.6	246.0	452.6	202.6	373.7	576.3
May	100.8	255.2	13.4	23.5	2.8	21.8	205.5	243.3	448.9	206.7	377.8	584.5
June	101.7	258.5	14.1	23.1	2.9	24.6	206.4	243.8	450.2	211.0	381.0	592.0
July	102.6	260.6	14.8	22.0	3.0	28.0	206.6	244.4	451.0	214.1	382.9	597.0
Aug	103.7	261.7	15.3	21.9	3.3	31.2	206.5	243.8	450.3	218.1	386.5	604.6
Sept	104.8	262.7	15.7	22.6	3.5	33.7	204.9	240.4	445.3	221.6	392.5	614.2
Oct	105.4	262.7	15.8	22.2	3.4	36.9	202.1	233.9	435.9	226.7	400.9	627.5
Nov	105.9	263.7	15.7	20.3	3.2	40.4	197.1	225.1	422.2	235.1	410.8	645.8
Dec	106.1	265.4	16.2	20.6	3.5	43.6	195.5	222.2	417.7	238.8	414.9	653.6
1980 Jan P	107.3	265.3	16.5	20.7	4.2	49.1	193.5	219.5	413.0	243.7	415.6	659.3
Feb P	108.2	268.1	16.5	21.7	3.3	56.8	190.9	214.6	405.5	249.5	419.7	669.2
Week ending:												
1980 Feb 6	108.2	269.0	16.5	21.2	3.2		192.1			247.3		
13	108.0	268.3	16.6	20.5	2.7		191.6			248.5		
20	108.3	269.3	16.6	22.8	3.5		190.8			249.6		
27	108.4	266.2	16.5	21.6	3.6		189.8			251.2		
Mar 5 P	108.7	265.8	16.8	22.2	3.7		188.5			252.0		
12 P	108.8	267.6	17.0	20.4	3.1		187.2			254.3		

187

Table A-3 (*Cont.*)

Year Month	Large-denomination time deposits			Term RPs[i]			Term Eurodollars net[k] NSA	Savings bonds	Short-term treasury securities[l]	Bankers accep-tances[m]	Com-mercial paper[n]
	At commercial banks[j]	At thrift institutions	Total	At commercial banks, not seasonally adjusted	At thrift institutions, not seasonally adjusted	Total, not seasonally adjusted					
1979 Feb	183.2	17.8	200.9	20.8	5.7	26.5	27.1	80.6	100.4	21.3	83.1
Mar	181.9	18.1	200.0	21.5	5.7	27.2	28.4	80.5	108.2	21.3	85.0
Apr	179.9	18.5	198.4	21.9	6.0	27.9	29.1	80.6	114.2	21.1	86.6
May	178.1	19.2	197.3	23.1	6.2	29.3	29.6	80.6	122.3	21.0	88.2
June	175.0	20.4	195.4	22.9	6.6	29.5	29.9	80.4	131.2	21.5	90.4
July	175.6	21.8	197.4	21.9	7.1	29.0	31.3	80.0	128.8	22.6	91.8
Aug	177.5	22.9	200.4	21.9	7.6	29.5	33.8	80.0	123.2	25.0	93.6
Sept	183.3	24.1	207.4	22.9	8.1	31.1	33.6	80.6	128.6	26.6	95.7
Oct	187.8	25.9	213.6	22.7	8.3	31.0	33.3	82.2	124.4	27.2	96.4
Nov	190.1	28.2	218.3	21.5	8.2	29.7	34.0	80.3	122.8	28.6	96.0
Dec	188.8	30.3	219.1	22.2	8.2	30.3	31.9	80.0	129.6	28.8	97.3
1980 Jan P	190.3	31.9	222.2	22.1	8.2	30.3	33.3	79.2	131.0	28.7	99.0
Feb P	193.3	33.3	226.6	21.2	8.1	29.3					
Week ending:											
1980 Feb 6	192.1			21.2							
13	192.9			23.3							
20	193.2			20.9							
27	193.1			20.5							
Mar 5 P	194.4			20.5							
12 P	193.9			20.3							

[a] Currency outside the U.S. Treasury, Federal Reserve Banks, and vaults of commercial banks.

[b] Demand deposits at commercial banks and foreign-related institutions other than those due to domestic banks, the United States government, and foreign banks and official institutions less cash items in the process of collection and Federal Reserve float.

[c] Includes ATS and NOW balances at all institutions, Credit Union share-draft balances, and demand deposits at mutual savings banks.

[d] Includes overnight and continuing-contract RPs issued to the nonbank public by commercial banks, net of amounts held by money market mutual funds.

[e] Issued by Caribbean branches of United States member banks to United States nonbank customers.

[f] Total money market shares outstanding.

[g] Small-denomination time deposits are those issued in amounts of less than $100,000.

[b] Large-denomination time deposits are those issued in amounts of $100,000 or more.

[i] Term RPs are those with original maturity greater than 1 day and exclude continuing contracts.

[j] Large-denomination time deposits at commercial banks less large time deposits held by money market mutual funds and thrift institutions.

[k] Term Eurodollars are those with original maturity greater than 1 day net of term Eurodollars held by money market mutual funds.

[l] Includes T-bills and coupons with remaining maturity of less than 18 months held by the nonbank public less such securities held by money market mutual funds.

[m] Net of bankers' acceptances held by accepting banks, Federal Reserve Banks, foreign official institutions, the Federal Home Loan Bank System, and money market mutual funds.

[n] Total commercial paper less commercial paper held by money market mutual funds.

SOURCE: *Federal Reserve Statistical Release H.6* (508), Mar. 21, 1980.

189

BIBLIOGRAPHY

Ayres, Leonard P.: *Turning Points in Business Cycles,* Augustus M. Kelly, New York, 1967.

Bolton, *Money, Investments and Profits,* Dow Jones Irwin, New York, 1967.

Edwards, Robert D., and John Magee: *Technical Analysis of Stock Trends,* John Magee, Springfield, Mass., 1957.

Friedman, M., and Swartz, *A Monetary History of the United States,* National Bureau of Economic Research, Princeton University Press, Princeton, N.J., 1963.

Homer, S.: *A History of Interest Rates,* Rutgers University Press, Rutgers, N.J., 1963.

The Interest Rate Forecast, BCA Publications, 1010 Sherbrooke St, W. Montreal, P.Q., Canada H3A 2R7 (monthly).

Mitchell, Wesley Clair: *Business Cycles and Their Cause,* University of California Press, Los Angeles, Calif., 1959.

Moore, Geoffrey H.: *Business Cycle Indicators,* vols. 1 and 2, National Bureau of Economic Research, Princeton University Press, Princeton, N.J., 1961.

Pring, Martin J.: *Technical Analysis Explained,* McGraw-Hill, New York, 1980.

Schumpeter, Joseph: *Business Cycles,* McGraw-Hill, New York, 1939.

Skinner, Dana: *Seven Kinds of Inflation,* McGraw-Hill, New York, 1937.

Sprinkel, Beryl W.: *Money and Markets,* Dow Jones Irwin, New York, 1971.

——— and Robert J. Genetski: *Winning with Money,* Dow Jones Irwin, New York, 1977.

INDEX